"Corey Taylor's *Th* consciously prepare ful, and his conte groundwork for creating spiritual, physical, emotional, and financial well-being!"

Bill D. Cordes MS
Professional Speaker, Author, Life Coach
Cordes Keynotes and Seminars

"In my opinion, when a man tells you his life story with a clear heart, you should pay attention. What Mr. Taylor shares in these pages is a personal story with both highs and lows. Learn from his experiences, hear his message, and grow. With faith and perseverance, you won't believe where you could get to. Become an *other 'aire.*"

Bret Rollins
Registered Principal
LPL Financial

"While reading many books, it is quite common to have the mind-set 'what's next?' and then to begin anticipating the next statement, thought, or the feel of the author. While reading this book, you will not experience this mind-set as it leaves no room for interpretation. It is practical and to the point and includes not only the poor but the middle class and the rich man. The contents of the book cause you to search your heart, see where you are good or bad, deal with it, and make the necessary adjustments. The information in the book contains nothing magical, just focus, discipline, self-control and some grind work. It will depend on where you are in life and enable you to become rich minded as you become rich monetarily."

Darnell Walker
College football coach and former NFL player

"Corey Taylor's *The Other 'aire* is a courageous and innovative piece of work that demonstrates the journey of a man who was able to overcome a life of obstacles and ultimately earn a life of comfort. But the greatest part of this journey was not achieving wealth but rather achieving the knowledge and wisdom that wealth is a virtual concept and not a determining factor for one's happiness. This is a true classic coming-of-age story."

Hicham Benkirane
Film Producer
Humanoids Inc./Clubdeal Ltd.

"Corey addresses some of the basics of financial management that I feel are essential for anyone searching for balance in their life. Corey's acknowledgement of where true happiness must be found is timeless."

Michael V. Ewy
President/CEO
Community State Bank

"Corey does a great job of presenting the American Dream. No matter the obstacles, don't give up."

Tad Jones
Majority Floor Leader
Oklahoma House of Reps 2009-10

"This book is a easy read! Some books drag along and it's sometimes difficult to pick up on what the author is trying to get across to the reader. NOT THIS BOOK! I tried putting this book down and I couldn't until I was finished. Corey Taylor gives hope to the up-and-coming and the well established in this book, through his life experiences. Great Book! Great Author! Loved it!"

Willie "PDUB" Moore, Jr.
President, Kingdom Music
Founder, Young Fly and Saved Entertainment

"Corey makes common 'cents' of financial woes and getting rich with his easy to read *The Other 'aire*. Corey provides insight from personal experiences we all share, mixed with colorful stories from his life. I read the book in less than two days, and after that, my son picked up it up and read it, too."

Kim Jackson
(Kimberly D. Flowers-Jackson)
Reporter
KTUL

THE OTHER 'AIRE

A REAL WORLD ALTERNATIVE
TO THE MILLIONAIRE

COREY D. TAYLOR

with
Shantele Lanos-Taylor

The Other 'aire:
A REAL WORLD ALTERNATIVE TO THE MILLIONAIRE
ISBN: 0-88144-348-4
Copyright © 2009 by Corey D. Taylor with Shantele Lanos Taylor,
Edited by Mia Wright
Printed by:

Camden House Books, LLC.
Post Office 727
Tulsa, Oklahoma 74133

DEDICATION

I would like to express my deepest gratitude and appreciation to the most important people in my life, my wife and children, without whose love and support this book would never have been written. *The Other 'aire* is dedicated to them, and to every other low-to-middle-income person who desires to get out of the rat race and experience real life, whether it be as a successful entrepreneur, an asset to their employer, or just a member of the human race living life to his/her highest potential.

*Understanding your past is essential
to obtaining a productive future...*

ACKNOWLEDGEMENTS

This book is the result of many hours of research and observation, and took years to put together. In it I share the knowledge I have accumulated during my lifetime and compiled for the purpose of helping others become more educated and enlightened in the areas of finance and success. I must admit, it was definitely a challenge for me. For years I had been asked to write a book that would speak to people in all walks of life and of varied financial backgrounds. For a long while I hesitated, not feeling qualified for the task. I finally came to realize that it was absolutely necessary as I could no longer sit back and watch people being taken in by "get rich quick" schemes.

In addition, part of my motivation was the fact that often after speaking at conferences and workshops, young people would ask me to leave materials, such as CDs or books, that would help them put into practice the principles I had shared with them. I was also encouraged by members of my church to write about true prosperity, and how I had always been blessed with a stream of wealth. They made it very clear that I could not keep this information to myself.

My decision was finally made when many of my business colleagues voiced the same sentiments. One notable colleague, Miranda Collins, encouraged me to write down what I was instilling in the lives of the people around me. She helped me see that once I had most of the information on paper, all I needed to do was compile it. So, after so many years and the encouragement of so many people, I am now pleased to have officially completed my first book, which you now hold in your hands.

As with any effort of this kind, there have been several people who have encouraged me in my pursuit whom I would like to mention. For starters, Gary Slyvas gave me the opportunity to write the foreword of his book, *Speaking God*. And my own book would not be possible without the love and support of those closest to me, my family, to whom I owe a debt of gratitude: Elnora Moore, Rosemary Taylor-Wallace, and Edward Wallace, Joyce Lanos-Smith, Lawrence Lanos Jr., Schekii Lanos, Edward Taylor, Anthony Hoskins, Curtis Taylor, and my dear aunts and uncles.

Many other people contributed to the success of this book, whom I would also like to thank: Lou Ann Marlar, Sarah Marlar, Hicham Benkirane, Dave Jewett, Chris and Brandi Seals, Allan Burroughs, Ersin Pertain, Dr. Bill Hagans, Malachi Gross (Malachi Group Media and Business Consulting), Elder Mike and Deatrea Rose, and Brittaney McFarland.

Lennard Finley-Investments (partner), former GBN Church Members, Rebecca Dukstein, Karen Weimer,

Willie Moore Jr., and Kelli Matney, along with my spiritual parents, Mike and Maria Scourten. All of these people have made major investments in my development, both spiritually and practically. And I owe a great deal of honor and respect to Margie Thompson and Vernon and Peggy Holloway for inspiring and motivating me to pursue my dreams.

Lastly, I would like to thank the many other people who have contributed along the way, but whose names I may have forgotten to mention. You know who you are, and I thank you profusely, as you have been a very important part of my journey.

Base life on the whole
and not just the parts…

TABLE OF CONTENTS

FOREWORD

It is with a great sense of honor that I write the foreword to the book, *The Other 'aire: A Real World Alternative to the Millionaire.*

I have known the author, Corey Taylor, for many years. In fact, I met him when he and his wife were both enrolled as students in Coffeyville Community College. Over the years, Corey has matured to be a Spirit-filled Christian and a very productive citizen with a strong sense of family. He is creative and innovative, an educator, businessman, and entrepreneur, full of enthusiasm, and worthy to author such a great book as *The Other 'aire.*

As I read *The Other 'aire,* I noted that the author vicariously shared a focus with the reader that is relevant and realistic. Taylor shares and speaks to today's generation about the pitfalls and mind-sets of poverty. He offers direction to the reader with a wholesome, holistic focus about life and true prosperity. By sharing nuggets of knowledge and quotations, the author makes his material readable and understandable. The reader will find numerous examples that will assist in life pursuits and purposes in gaining a little more out of life.

I believe that all who read *The Other 'aire* will experience insightful truths and valuable principles that will transform their thinking and their lives. It is truly a work of inspiration.

Virgil O. Horn, Jr., MS, Th.D.
Mayor of Coffeyville, Kansas

The Other 'aire is a conceptual premise that can lay the foundational framework in one's quest for success. It challenges the poverty-minded and negates pessimism. It voids any and all excuses for not obtaining and/or fulfilling one's true purpose/mission in life.

In today's economic slump, this book offers inspiration and hope. It is timely. It gives the reader practical principles and realistic nuggets of truth as it walks through and shares personal testimonials of the author. Corey Taylor shares both his failures and successes. He is transparent in his delivery and models both the pitfalls and joys of financial literacy, or lack thereof. He uses the "simple things to confound the wise."

The Other 'aire, in and of itself, is a tool of inspiration and motivation. It is inclusive, not exclusive. It is a qualifying agent that should equip the reader with the tools necessary to be productive and financially stable. It is a qualitative term that is intended to edify one's personal esteem and being.

Challenged by life's obstacles, Corey has managed to defy the odds and follow the path less taken. He has overcome a life of hardship and poverty, and offers counsel to those who are less fortunate and to those who try to live the fast-paced life. The author shares stories/parables to illustrate commonality of events. Leadership studies through Pittsburg State University provided transforming insight as to how "looking through different sets of lenses" can change one's perspective on life.

These lenses merely represent focal points shaped by personal life experiences. It is imperative that one looks outside his/her own spectrum of reality and see the bigger picture!!!! If one only focuses on the traumatic and/or sad events, it is difficult to move forward. This applies to finances, as well. If one only recalls the penny-pinching days of poverty and pawnshops, goals of being out of debt and owning a home can seem quite lofty and unattainable.

Shantele T. Taylor, MS

To know truth is to be wise,
to LIVE truth is to be brave...

Preface

Every writer of a book on financial success has a story to tell. While they do discuss their struggles with financial lack to some degree, they usually concentrate more on the "rags to riches" aspect of their lives than on actually giving you the tools you need to get out of poverty. This book, however, is different, in that the author takes you on a journey to the depths of his family's struggle with poverty and actually shows you how to achieve success over your financial lack.

The author's story will ignite a passion in you as you journey with him from his humble beginnings, through his liberation from governmental welfare, to the actualization of what personal financial success is all about. The culmination of the events of his life led him to the realization that being a billionaire or millionaire is not the only measure of financial success in life, and that there has been way too much pressure placed on people becoming millionaires or greater in today's society. After reading countless books and doing years of research, which resulted in innumerable failures, he began to believe that there was no alternative to happiness other than being rich. He found that society imposes the belief that being rich is the only way to happiness. After spending much time feeling help-less and depressed about his inability to reach the million-aire status, the author made a shocking discovery which presented itself to him in the form of a question. "Why do I have to be a millionaire or rich to be happy?" After much thought and internal debating, the author coined a phrase that seemed to epitomize his newfound hope. That phrase was *other 'aire.*

OTHER 'AIRE:

A person who has the same characteristics and habits of the rich, but their financial worth has not yet reached the monetary value of a million dollars.

The author realized, just as there are steps in education, like from high school to community college and then on to the university level, there are similar steps for financial success. These steps are: poverty, other 'aire, millionaire, and beyond. And the author wants to make one thing very clear, that the middle class and the other 'aire are not the same step. He realized this truth because he made it to the middle class and peaked. There is truly a middle class, but the other 'aire class is a class all by itself.

Other 'aire

Other 'aire: A person who has the same characteristics and habits of the rich, but their financial worth has not yet reached the monetary value of a million dollars.

To make a journey, one must prepare;

to complete it, one must have heart...

CHAPTER ONE

OVERVIEW

THE OTHER 'AIRE IS A BOOK for the everyday average person who wants a little more out of life; these are people who strive for happiness, joy, financial freedom, and mental clarity. When all these elements are properly aligned, it makes a world of difference in their lives. Now, some people suffer from low self-esteem and don't think they amount to anything because, after all, they are not rich and seem to go through a cycle of meaningless daily events. This book will highlight a different way of living for those who are tired of a mediocre life. I used to be a person who bought into the idea that I had to have a million dollars to be happy and make a difference in this world. After a lifetime of pursuing this goal to no avail, I finally figured out that I didn't need that at all. In fact, I began to see that if I was patient, lived my life, and was purposefully content, riches would eventually come my way.

It is sad to admit that today's society promotes and puts way too much emphasis on being extremely wealthy. This is not realistic for everyone. In fact, this dangerous way of thinking has caused a great deal of destruction in people's lives, because they are doing whatever they can to get rich, such as playing the lottery, gambling, and getting into debt. Society has pushed the envelope on setting the norms. At a time when the citizens of this country should be helping each other to become better citizens, they simply leave it to the ultra rich to dictate how the rest of us should live our lives. As a result, millions of people are doing whatever they can to get rich or die trying (literally), thinking that being extremely wealthy is the only way to achieve happiness.

I remember when the casinos first came to St. Louis, Missouri. People gambled away their homes thinking they were going to get rich on the casino boats. The news at that time was even reporting people jumping off bridges because they had gambled their lives away and lost everything they owned at the casinos. Now, my purpose is not to judge, but merely to point out that this is the same kind of insanity that our culture is promoting. I am not trying to tell anyone how to live their life, and certainly, if you have extra money to blow on this kind of entertainment, then by all means do your thing. But if you do not have this kind of extra, my advice would be not to spend hard earned money on the chance to get rich quick.

Although I am a dreamer and a very hard worker, it took me a while to realize that "all work and no play" made Corey a dull boy. Having fun is definitely a good thing. On the other hand, I don't want anyone reading this book to believe that I am advocating laziness. I am also not a believer in the *Robin Hood* method of "stealing from the rich to give to the poor." Contrarily, I believe that the *other* 'aires should be given the same latitude as the rich to make and hold onto their money and be symbols of wealth.

You've probably already gathered that this book is not full of "get rich quick" schemes. Once you have read it in its entirety, you will have a new perspective regarding life and finances. Please don't be misled into believing you will get rich just by reading a book. You also have to apply the information I am sharing with you in order to get the benefit. I can attest to that because I have read many books and ventured into all kinds of different business opportunities through both reading and practical application.

Now, some may say I did not know what I was doing, and that's why I gave up on many of the ventures I got involved in. But I assure you that is not the truth at all. I simply traded sanity for insanity. I tried everything from multilevel network marketing schemes to opening my own clothing stores. Neither of these ventures worked for me. You too can try them, but I recommend that you read this book first. My point is not to discourage you. These businesses may work for you — they just did not work for me. Truthfully, I got tired of chasing after everyone else's dream and making them rich. If you get involved with a multilevel marketing business, common sense will finally show you that you are helping someone else get rich. There is a great possibility that, even with all your hard work, the promised wealth may never come for you. Still, there are many people who have been successful in network marketing. Just make sure it is a fit for you.

By the way, have you ever noticed that these network marketing businesses want you to buy into them with money and then they promise to make you rich? Rich people make money through their visions, dreams, and passions, not by buying a whole a lot tapes, CDs and books. For most network marketing companies, these books and CDs are just another way for them to make money. I thought these tapes, books and CDs held some type of magical power to make me rich, but I soon realized that there is no substitute for hard work and vision. Books are great and we should read them, but there comes a point when you must be responsible and take action for your own future. A lot of things can be promised, but if you don't put effort and knowledge behind what you're doing, then you are just wasting your time.

My purpose is to give you hope, especially with the U.S. economy on the verge of possible collapse. This book will serve as a "cookbook" of sorts, providing recipes and guidelines on how to bring different elements together to make one successful product. As with a bread recipe, most people need a "start" and then they can take it from there. Think of this book as that "start." By the time you finish, you'll be properly equipped to make a better life!

Other 'aires are people who start out with a poverty-stricken mentality, but have an innate drive in them that tells them they can have a better life. When I use the term "poverty-stricken," I am not just talking about the poor. I'm referring to anyone who is in debt and doesn't have a financial plan for their future. In addition, *other 'aires* are people who realize that integrity is a vital key to success in life.

Before I go any further, I must define the term "integrity." It is simply doing what is right, even when no one is watching you; it is upholding your promises and keeping true to your word. It means you can be trusted above all, and it is a necessary survival tool. I used to be a man without integrity. At times I still struggle with this virtue, but one of the keys I've learned is to keep pressing on until I get a skill mastered. Operating in integrity helps you to maximize your life.

How many times have you listened to the conversations of millionaires and billionaires? It may seem as if they are the only kinds of people who bring any value to the table of life, but this is the biggest misconception in the marketplace today. Now don't misunderstand me. I like to hear what millionaires and billionaires have to say, but truthfully, it is the poor and middle class of this world who make it go round. They play a huge part in driving the economy. You can see how, even in this crisis period, governments are urging people to continue to spend their money. If the middle class stopped buying things and working their crazy jobs, America would not really be America. So, yes it is good to hear rich people's stories, but I constantly have to remind myself that my life doesn't revolve around them, and neither should yours.

While I am in no way trying to discredit these "*aires*," I just want you to understand that you are still very valuable, even if you have not attained their same monetary status. We are all some type of '*aire*. The suffix "-aire" actually comes from the French language. For instance, when you speak of a millionaire, it simply describes a person who counts their money in increments of tens of thousands – one who has ten hundred thousands. The suffix itself has no special significance, then. It is the word in front of it that makes it important, such as billion, million, legion, or concession. So, let's add a new term to your vocabulary – *other 'aire*. I coined this term because I have come to believe that people have wealth in more ways than just millions or billions of dollars. The primary focus of *other 'aires* is finding out just how valuable they are, not just how much money they have, which paves the pathway for wealth to eventually come.

Now, I am going to share a truth with you that you may not be ready to receive. Okay, here it goes. Everyone… won't… be… a… millionaire! I know, I know, this is a shock, but at least you can get over it now and move on with your life.

There is a passage in the Bible that says, "For it is God who gives you the knowledge to obtain wealth." Now, I'm not here to tell you who's going to be rich, because anyone can be rich if they put their mind to it. But the reality is that not everyone will be a millionaire. I remember watching a Steven Segal movie years ago in which he played a doctor who was trying to find the cure for a virus that was killing people in this small town. His father, a Native American shaman, said one of the most profound lines I had ever heard in a film. In response to his son's frustration at not being able to find the cure, the shaman said, "You should just rest and the cure will come to you." Wow! Have you ever lost something and couldn't find it until you stopped looking – only to find that it was right in front of your face the whole time? Similarly, most of us are trying so hard to find money, not realizing it's been right in front of our faces. In our frantic, haphazard search, we have overlooked it time and time again.

Jesus Himself said the poor you will always have among you [Matthew 26:11]. Don't take my word for it. Turn your TV on and you will see that there are too many poor people to change that fact about the world. Simply put, we will always have poor people. Now, once we get the knowledge of how to get out of poverty, we should pass that knowledge to others.

Back when I had my clothing business, I remember flying to Las Vegas for the "The Magic Show." This was an event that showcased the latest fashion trends, which many vendors like myself attended. During my flight, I got into a conversation with a man named Zack, taking advantage of a potential networking opportunity. As we talked, I realized that Zack and I were in the same business. He was a Middle Eastern gentleman who owned three stores. I shared with him my ambition to build an empire of stores. I sat, listening in amazement to his wisdom. Jealousy seemed to be a common characteristic of the people we associated with through our businesses.

He told me about a strange encounter he once had with a man. Each of them were sharing about the successes of their respective businesses and how many stores they each had. In the middle of the conversation, the man angrily shouted at Zack saying, "Why do you have so many stores and I only have one?" My new friend was shocked at the man's response and replied, "God gives one man the power and ability to fill one cup of water and another man ten cups of water. So, don't be mad at me if you're only able to fill one cup and I'm able to fill ten. Just be happy and do your best, and maybe more will come."

So many people that write books would have you believe that everyone is going to be rich. This is simply not true. In fact, in order for you to be rich, you have to be willing to make a lot of changes your behavior. Even if you already see yourself as an *other 'aire*, you will still need to make changes. You have to be willing to open your understanding to realities that you may never have thought about. Be encouraged, because you are never too old to change.

NUGGET:

Quit beating yourself up because you did not become rich (or whatever else – fill in the blank) by a certain age.

That story my new friend shared with me really made an impression. The vivid picture Zack painted with his words helped my understanding. His story actually made me feel better about life. I use this story quite frequently to motivate myself and others.

Each of us was put on this earth for a reason. No matter how great or how small, your life is significant. Most of us ignore our true purpose in the hopes of finding "untold" riches which we think will be the answer to our problems. The reason these riches are "untold" is because no one has ever seen them! That's a fairytale. The real problem is that most of us don't want to find our own way anymore. We would rather have someone else tell us what to do and how to do it. Hard work is out of the question and problem solving is next to impossible.

Our society has created a group of people solely dependent on millionaires telling us how to live, instead of really living our own lives. Just because someone is rich doesn't mean they are qualified to tell the rest of us how to live. Rich people do not all come from the same set of circumstances. We need to realize that there are different strokes for different folks. Now, please don't use what I am saying as an excuse to not try, but as a step to go out and have that good life.

NUGGET:

Life is about exploration and all of us have a purpose; it just takes some of us longer to find ours.

We place so much emphasis on being rich or a millionaire that we are slowly declining into greed and self-loathing. This is where integrity comes into play. The hallmark of integrity is your word – your word helps create your credit worthiness. Without this, you pay an awful lot to do a little bit of nothing. Without credit worthiness, you are forced to pay very high prices. Integrity is doing what's right with the money you've borrowed. Most financial books on the market tell you to stay away from credit, but, unless you are rich, you need credit or a life's savings. It should be used as a tool for your success. True *other 'aires* understand this and are secure in the use of credit for specific purposes.

NUGGET:

Credit is not a magic pot of gold,

but a means to accomplish an end.

Remember, *other 'aires* are everyday people who just want a little bit more out of everyday life. To have that, you have to educate yourself about finances and business, because we are involved with them on a daily basis.

Are you aware that money in any form can make you rich? Check this out: Pennies, nickels, dimes, quarters, and dollars will all make you rich, if you have enough of them. So, the difference between you, the poor person, and a rich person is simply your mind-set. We are all able to dig in the same backyard. We all live in the same world physically, but the way we see the world is distinctly different.

I don't care how you divide up a million dollars, it is still made up of a combination of the aforementioned currencies. The issue at stake is that millionaires know how to maintain and/or make more money, while the *other 'aire* is learning this process. The *other 'aire* oftentimes does not have the benefit of inheriting generational financial wisdom or good stewardship skills. They have to learn this process from beginning to end, many times bumping their heads and making plenty of mistakes along the way. If we don't learn the proper use of money, we can never hope to change our behavior.

Money is a tool that is used to support livelihood, a medium of exchange. If an *other 'aire* wants to start making more money, then some things are going to have to change in his/her mind-set. It means that we will have to fully discipline and train ourselves in money management. *Other 'aires* are people in transition. They are on their way to being holistically wealthy in every area of their lives.

So, I have a question that I want you to ponder. With there being so much talk about millionaires and billionaires, does one have to have millions to be happy? Why can't a person making 50k, 100k, or even 300k a year be just as satisfied with life as a millionaire? We cannot escape the commercialization of the millionaires, and that is creating big problems for people everywhere. There are so many people trying to live the "lifestyle of the rich and famous" that casinos and lotteries are gaining more ground all over the country. Everyone wants to hit that big number, that big jackpot! You can see it on every TV channel, bookstore, and in every advertisement.

In the book *Rich Dad, Poor Dad,* Robert Kiyosaki makes a great statement about what he was taught. He said his rich dad told him that it is not how much you make, but it's how much you get to keep. Wow! So, can *other 'aires* be just as successful and satisfied as millionaires? The answer is... emphatically... YES! Even if you don't make a million, do the best that you can with what you have and you will still be all right. That is exactly what Zack was saying. If you reach for the sky, at least you are no longer on the ground running with the turkeys. Instead, you are soaring with the eagles, even if you don't fly that high.

I am glad to be an *other 'aire.* If I become a millionaire, that's good. But, if I don't, it's not going to kill me! I am encouraging you to reevaluate your life. There are so many stories of people who went out looking for gold (remember the gold rush?) and many of them died in the process. Well, I don't want anyone to die trying to get rich. I am a firm believer that if it is meant for you to be rich, it will definitely happen.

I know that what I'm saying may make some people mad. However, enough is enough. Let's stop the madness! We are fast becoming a society of ultra greedy people doing whatever we can just to become rich. I can attest I pushed myself for years, trying to become a millionaire, and then one day it hit me. What if I only ended up being a *pennyaire, hundredaire, or thousandaire?* Would that really be so bad? Would that make me worth less than the millionaire? Perhaps in terms of money, but in my personal wealth — I think not. Too often the media makes us feel like we are unimportant if we are not filthy rich.

Now, I know that some prosperity people are not going to like this, but it's the truth. Being rich isn't only about the money, even though money is part of the driving force that makes it happen. But it is better to pursue a better quality of life than to chase after money. Let me reiterate that there is nothing wrong with having money. But my question is: What do you do with it once you get it?

NUGGET:

Sound is to a motion picture what money is
to life; it's nice to hear the soundtrack,
but even better to see the movie!

I recently heard someone at a conference say, "Money is rated high, like air and water. You need it to survive." I believe that is true. If it weren't, no one would work or put such a great value on money. Everything costs something!

Why can't everyone be a millionaire? Let's take a look at the ecosystem for an explanation. In an ecosystem everything feeds off of something. Example: Worms eat dirt. A bird comes along and eats the worm. The cat eats the bird. The cat dies and decays back into dirt and then the cycle starts again.

So, just like the ecosystem, human beings have economics. Economics operate on a similar system except you have the "haves" and the "have-nots." The "have-nots" keep making the "haves" richer. Let me break it down. People buy "bling" at a jewelry store, and the retail jeweler purchased the bling from a wholesaler and the wholesaler gets it from the manufacturer, and the manufacturer gets it from the diamond mines in Africa. After all these middle men, you realize that you are paying a lot of money, because they get to set the price. You may be saying, "I don't get this," but in fact you do. The "haves" are not called the "haves" for nothing. They are called "haves" because not only do they have, but they also have a means of getting things done. So, the haves go and buy their things from other haves, not from the "have-nots." They have a good system and there is nothing wrong with them having a system. The tragedy is that the poor and middle class don't educate themselves like the haves do. They have a different value and education system than we do. As I said earlier, they think differently than we do. So, I hope you can see this reality that I am about to show you.

The "haves" are always in control, and most "have-nots" buy their goods from the haves. It is a smart system. You've heard it said before, the rich get richer while the poor get poorer. You can pull out your violin now. I know, you want me to tell you that you have been cheated, but I can't do that because you haven't. It's not too late for you to get educated and get yours. Don't play crazy and act like someone owes you something. No one owes you anything unless they took something from you and most of the time this is not the case. It is usually a perceived taking.

Oh, if you are poor or middle class, take a hard look at your spending habits and behavior, and see if they don't have something to do with your situation. In essence, "the haves" have learned to be financially smart. Anyone can be smart, but being financially smart takes discipline and hard work. If the "have-nots" don't change their mind-sets, they will always have-not. I hope you realize that this system is not going to stop for you or me. It will continue going on just as it always has. What we need is to learn how the system operates and make it work for us. *Other 'aires* don't just sit back, but take this type of knowledge by the horns and make things happen for themselves.

NUGGET:

Systems can only take advantage
of the ignorance of the ignorant.

They don't just sit around waiting for someone to give them a handout because handouts won't teach you anything. Stop falling prey to your own ignorance. Learn the system and make it work for you.

Another concept of the *other 'aire* is to be prepared to win the battle. You have to arm yourself with the right knowledge. No system is perfect. I want you to say that to yourself fifty times until you get it in your head. "No system is perfect." If you understand that no system is perfect, then you can see that there are exceptions to the rules or what most people call "loopholes." These loopholes will help you see a different reality that is not seen by all. Only the people with insight can see these loopholes and insight about loopholes come from education. So, if the system is flawed, then learn it, work it, use it, and you will come out on top. Don't sit there and whine about it anymore or I am going to have to bring you some crackers to have with that whine. LOL!

NUGGET:

Learn it, use it, work it, and top it.

Well, there are more new and exciting ideas to explore in the chapters ahead. Attention to everyone reading this book: You are an *other 'aire,* even if you don't know it yet! You are one because you are daring enough to read this book. You have what it takes to be successful. You may say, "How do you know that?" The very title of this book stresses the possibility of your future. You may not be a millionaire or billionaire, but there is a class for you.

Other 'aires are everywhere. They are in business, social work, law, sanitation, etc. The *other 'aire* understands money, but their purpose in life is not to get rich. If they just happen to bump into riches while they are living, that's great. In order to be an *other 'aire,* you are going to have to find your place and your purpose in life. With that knowl- edge, the rest is, as they say, history. An *other 'aire* knows how to manage money and life. And *other 'aires* are not just anybody. They are warriors in their lives and in the lives of other people.

Why don't you set aside some time and join this highly motivated and elite group of everyday people who just want a little more out of life? Allow me to assist you in pursuing your purpose, and making a wonderful plan for your life. Become an *other 'aire* today.

CHAPTER TWO

LEARNING WITHOUT APPLICATION

WITH SO MUCH FOCUS on being a millionaire or billionaire in today's society, isn't it a wonder that more ordinary people aren't just giving up on life and calling it quits? I say this because when one person is talking about making a million dollars, it does not seem like reality to those who are barely getting by. So many have felt the pressure to become millionaires. For some people, it is too far out of their reach. I coined the phrase *other 'aire* to help people see a different reality for resolving their financial problems.

Others have even taken the word "millionaire" and made variations on it, like "reallionaire," a phrase coined by Dr. Pharr Gray. I had the pleasure of meeting Dr. Gray and a group of young people who had been impacted by his work with youth. I met him for the first time in February 2007, in upstate New York. As I sat and listened to this most impressive young man, I knew it was time to overcome my fears and do what I felt like I was supposed to do in life. I figured if he could do it, I could too. Listening to him talk I realized that all we do is just listen to people talk. It is time for everyone to get up and do something, instead of just listening as other people tell us what to do. If we don't start a new conversation about making it in life, people will find themselves overcome by grief and misery, and of course, misery does love company.

So, I guess it's time we clear the air. LOL! So many writers want you to believe that they have the magic goose egg to make you rich. But, what they fail to tell their readers is that building riches takes skill and drive, unless you've inherited your money like Paris Hilton. No offense to Ms. Hilton, but it's not rocket science to realize that money begets money.

The average person doesn't need to be filthy rich to be happy. I am a living example of that. I am happy, but I still work hard to be successful, even though I may not be what's considered "rich." The reason I am happy is because I live for a purpose.

I bet you're as tired as I am of hearing about millionaires. I'm not saying that there is anything wrong with being a millionaire – I just don't want you to waste the rest of your life trying to be one and miss out on life. If you do that, chances are you will end up miserable. Before I go any further, though, I want to give you an understanding about millionaires. I have found in my research that if a person truly knows what they are looking for, they will find it. So, what I want you to do is follow me so that I can give you some understanding as to how you can start changing your outlook on life. The reason why so many people are writing about being millionaires is because so many people want to be rich and don't understand that being rich is much more than having money.

Let's take a closer look at word construction. I will say it again: the word "millionaire" is actually one word with a suffix. The suffix of this word is -aire. This would be the same suffix that is added to words such as billionaire, millionaire, reallionaire, and legionnaire. When this suffix is added to a word, intimidation immediately sets in. But millionaires are human too – they, eat, drink, sleep, and work like you and me. The only difference is that they just think differently than the majority of us. We will get into more detail on that in another chapter.

All the aforementioned words have one thing in common, which is the suffix -aire. If you are tired of hearing about them, then get ready, because I want to drive this point home. You have the right to things just like these other 'aires. Do not forget that you are an *other 'aire.*

NUGGET:

We are all aires of something;

we just need to figure out what.

Dr. Gray's book is called *Reallionaire.* Now, digest that for a minute. We can all be -aires of being real because life is real and that's what we have. Again, million and billion are simply root words with -aire as the suffix. If the root word is what's important, and it is, then can't a person be a thousand-aire or hundred-aire? I used to tell people that my wife and I started off as *hundred-aires* and then *thousand-aires,* and now we are on our way to millionaire. However, this is no longer our goal. I must confess, it was because I had always wanted the millionaire status, not my wife. I finally got so tired of chasing money without obtaining it, that I decided that if it was meant to be, it would happen.

My wife and I started off on welfare sixteen years ago, but things look very different to us now, because we've learned to see things differently. One of the things that had to happen is we had to be willing to change our mindset and see ourselves as victors instead of victims. When I used to tell people that I was a hundred-aire, they would laugh at me. Well, guess what? They are not laughing anymore. People may think it is silly to say that you are a hundred-aire, but it motivated us to pass that level and keep striving for more. I have had opportunities to be around rich people and many of them believe that there is a difference in humanity when they become rich. However, it is simply not true. To be fair to rich people, I know that not all of them believe they are superior to the poor. Truthfully, I can't blame rich people for feeling this way because some of us have contributed to their attitudes as well.

For instance, when I was younger it was easy for me to blame others for their shortcomings, and their reluctance to change their mind-set. But after you read this book you will not play that blame game anymore. In order for a person's mind to change, you have to be willing to examine your thought processes, and to admit that maybe you need to think differently. So, it's time to get rid of that "stinking thinking." Negative, poverty mentality keeps people from becoming millionaires. If a poor person truly knew what they had, they would realize they have the potential to be rich as well. The challenge is that non-millionaires don't realize what they already have. I mean, if you are an able-bodied worker you can have any type of life you want, but it will take some hard work and application.

For years I read books and listened to CDs by Dave Ramsey, Myles Munroe, T. D. Jakes, Robert Kiyosaki, Darrell Andrews, and many others. I read and read and read until my brain was about to bust open with all the information I was putting into my head. However, there does come a time when a student must apply the knowledge he has received during his studies. If this is your case and you have been a student for a long time, it is time to get out of the books and spread your wings and fly. But the only person who can make you fly is you.

Having knowledge and putting it into practice are two very different things. We were all created to do something; the trick is to figure out what that thing is for you. I like to joke with people by telling them I am still trying to figure out what I want to do when I grow up. It can be a long process figuring out what you want to do. When I say that, I am not talking about knowing exactly what you are going to do for the rest of your life, but about being honest enough with yourself to acknowledge that some things are going to have to change if you want your life to be different than it is at present.

It has always been rather amusing to me that people sometimes think they are the only ones experiencing frustration. They should be happy to know that they are among a very diverse group of people. Even after reading a lot of books and going to college, we all want to give up from time to time. I want to shatter some of the myths and tell you the truth.

Another thing most people don't realize is that there is more than one way to get rich. However, the real ways are rare and they are roads less traveled. When opportunities arrive for you to buy books and tapes, you need to know that you must make wise decisions. Although there are some good authors out there, don't go broke by making every author rich because you like collecting books and not doing anything with them. Make a change in your mentality TODAY. Be determined that this is your season. Quit making everyone else rich and focus on being a better you.

I can remember being on that trip in New York that I mentioned earlier when I heard Dr. Gray's speech. His advice was to "find your purpose." Now that wasn't the first time I had heard that; I'd heard the same from others like Myles Munroe and T. D. Jakes. But something clicked in my mind when he asked, "What were you put on this earth to do?" Wow! Now that gave me real pause to reflect. I thought to myself, *How many times have I heard this stuff, without realizing what was going on?* Something definitely changed for me after I heard that question. I had a mental, emotional, and spiritual eclipse that I did not anticipate. It was as if everything I had studied, learned, and taught came together and I knew it was time to put away the books and put the knowledge into action. It was easy to listen because he is younger than I, and he had made a million dollars at fifteen years old. That day unlocked something in me that has catapulted me to another level of success in my life.

NUGGET:

Most of the time, when you hear people speak

about something and you respond to it, rarely

is it anything new to you. It may be that at

this particular moment, you are open to believe it.

Many times, our inner beings may be closed off to the possibilities of what's being taught. The reason you have responded this time is very simple, but the answer will amaze you. Through research and observation I have discovered that a person can hear information over and over and retain it, but not apply it. It's not until one actually applies the information they have learned and makes mistakes in application that the true learning process begins. As a result of the mistakes made, the information previously received but not believed becomes viable resource to draw from. This creates a formula for success.

I believe we are in an age where it is absolutely essential for everyone to learn good financial management skills. The world as we know it is not getting any better, and we need to be fully equipped if we are going to survive. We have to educate ourselves. We can't let the rappers and the politicians do our thinking for us. We are in the age of accountability. This means, "Go[al] MINE" your own business.

Now, I don't want to beat a dead horse with this story, but there was one more thing I heard that lit up a serious light bulb in my head as Dr. Gray spoke that day. He implied, "It is not totally up to you to find your own purpose in life. Find out what other people say you're good at and 'goal mine' that special quality because it may be your pay horse." I had never heard this idea expressed quite like that. He may not have intended it or the people may not have caught on, but he was talking about a concept I call "goal mining." "Goal mining" is digging up your future endeavors and making them concrete. Simply put, if people say you are good at something, then VALUE IT and MAKE IT your product.

Now that you have this tool in your repertoire, you are more equipped to do great things and create riches. You must find your purpose, but what other people say about you will help you narrow down what you are good at. In order for this to happen, you must be willing to listen to the truth. If people see your purpose and help you narrow it down by telling you what you are good at, then you will have a product people are more likely to desire. This will help you market and create a greater demand for what you have to offer. In marketing, word of mouth has always been the best tool for product advertisement.

Without realizing it, you are probably already in your business. Business ventures start off with ideas, and ideas can easily translate into money. As I said earlier, money will not solve all your problems, but it will help one of the biggest problems, which is being broke. Hey, I realize that reading this book is only a small step in the process of eliminating your financial woes. Nevertheless, it is a step. The good thing is, we will now listen if people say we are good at something. Their words encourage us to keep moving forward and perfecting our product, and eventually marketing it.

After you perfect and package your gift, you will have a marketable product. What's exciting about this is that the very ones who inspired and motivated you to package your gift will be the ones to purchase it and even help you sell it! Don't be afraid to ask them for help when you are trying to sell yourself as a product. There is no shame in asking for help. Moving forward with your gift will stop all the foolish talk of the naysayers. You have a purpose, so why not live it to its fullest? You can live an abundant life by discovering new dimensions of your purpose every day. I love what the Good Book says about this: "Seek ye first the kingdom of heaven and his righteousness, and everything else shall be added unto you." I do believe in God's provisions, and as you step forward in your purpose, He opens doors.

If you look around and see many things,
you are observant;
if you see nothing, you are blind...

CHAPTER THREE

THE SCHOOL OF OBSERVATION

M. WALKER IS A DEAR FRIEND of mine who played professional football for over five years. I can remember when he got signed to the NFL. I was so excited for us and what we had accomplished. After all, we had worked so hard to get where we were.

Have you ever done this before – ride on someone else's fame, after they worked the long hours? Well, I did that very thing and thought I was justified in riding on his dreams. In my mind, it was okay because we were friends, best buddies. Because I had helped him out in college, I thought that he owed me something.

Now, before we go any further, let's make sure that all those chips that you are carrying on your shoulders are removed, just like I had to remove the ones on mine. Otherwise, you will go down the wrong road and blame other people for your mistakes and failures. Now, don't you go getting mad at me. At one point or another, we all have had a chip on our shoulders, envying the success of the rich.

Although this may be difficult to hear, another key to success is not only getting the chips off your shoulders, but taking a good look at reality. Most people who want to move ahead in life will eventually want the chips off their shoulders, but it is not enough to just want them off, or to want someone else to remove them. We must take them off ourselves. So many young people probably won't understand this terminology, but what I'm saying is that many of them think that the world owes them something. As already stated in the previous chapter, we need to apply information, not just get head knowledge. Without applying the lessons we learn, we fail to grasp the basic concept of educating ourselves. Many of us don't want the hard truth, we just want other people to tell us what to do without us cooperating with the process. Life is about survival of the fittest in mind, emotion, spirit and intellect. If you don't believe me, then stay where you are. I promise you, you will be left in poverty and in the dust. If you don't have knowledge and the ability to adapt, you will die. The same goes for feeding your wholeness, and growing in the areas where you are lacking. If you don't like where you are, and if you don't get out of what you are in, then you will die. Please be wise – hear and analyze these truths I am sharing.

Now, let me get back to my own story. I was very happy for my friend Marquis, as well as myself, because I thought that we would come up together. I thought his success would be my success. And he wasn't the only friend I felt this way about; I tried to live my dreams through other friends as well. I know that I am not the only one who has done this. Because I was caught up in all the excitement, I failed to realize that Marquis was doing all the work. I mean, it was Marquis who went to practice, got hit on the field, and took the injuries associated with the sport. I did not want to go through any of that. I didn't want to put forth the "guts," but I did want the glory. And I see this same thing occurring often. In fact, if you watch TV, you will see that almost everyone is trying to get rich off their friends without investing in themselves. You'll notice that a lot of rappers' friends are getting piggyback rides. I guess it's okay, if the rappers themselves don't mind.

But the valuable lesson I learned from this "piggybacking" experience with Marquis is that I was scared to seek out success for myself because doing things for myself required courage and guts. At the time I thought I had these qualities, but I was sadly mistaken! I came to realize this after Marquis was signed to the St. Louis football team, and then was traded to the Washington D.C. team. For a while, I was still able to see Marquis he was traded, but then I found myself becoming mad and scared. I was fearful because I thought that Marquis would no longer desire my friendship due to his newly found success. The hard truth was that I was afraid that Marquis would be wealthy and I would remain poor. Ouch!

After several months, Marquis asked me to go shopping with him and a mutual friend at the Galleria Mall in St. Louis. During my visit, they both cornered me and asked, "Why are you scared of being successful?" Now, my immediate reaction was, "No way! I'm not afraid!" But, they were able to see the truth and they confronted me about my lying. I have to admit, that was one of those pivotal moments in my life, and it helped me face one of the main things that was holding me back from success. From that point on, I was determined not to be afraid of being successful. Even after my friends' scrutiny, I thought I had the answer, but I didn't. What I now realize is that it was just the start of my journey and my schooling to find the wealthy me. You see, it wasn't "we," but "me." It wasn't Marquis's or anyone else's responsibility to take care of me. It was my responsibility to find my own success.

A couple of years passed and Marquis invited me to watch him play San Francisco. He played for Oakland and his brother Darrell played for San Francisco. I had to drum up a little money to fly to Oakland but Marquis paid for the majority of the trip. I had no idea what I would experience. At this point in my life, I had not had a taste of many of the finer things life had to offer (but, boy, was I getting ready to!). I found myself back in school with Marquis again, along with my newest teacher, Darrell Walker (or "Ol' Dude" as he was called). They quickly started teaching me, and let me tell you, I was all ears.

The first thing I remembered was going to Fisherman's Wharf and them buying fresh crabs. I mean, live and boiled fresh. I was amazed as they spent money like it was no problem. I must admit, I felt embarrassed because I didn't have that type of money, and at this part of my journey to wealth, I was trying to live within my own means and not in my friends' shadows. After we bought the lobster, I can remember commenting, "Aren't you all spending too much money for just a meal?" Darrell turned to Marquis and asked, "What's wrong with 'Big C'?" Then he looked at me and said, "You can't be ghetto all your life! It's time for a change!" Wow! What he was really saying to me was to stop thinking with a poverty-stricken mentality.

That was an eye-opening trip and it would not be the last class I would have with Marquis and Darrell. A year later while we were back in St. Louis, we got into a discussion about assets, wealthy people, and delayed gratification. Marquis and Darrell began the conversation by talking about NFL players and how they leased mostly everything. Darrell said, "It doesn't make sense. Once the NFL life is over, we need to have assets."

The term "assets" was a totally new term for me at that time. Even though I had earned two degrees from accredited colleges, my mentality was limited due to my personal experience.

You can go to college all day every day and major in finance, but that doesn't necessarily mean you are financially literate! This should turn on another light bulb in your life! As you have probably guessed, even though I went to college, I was financially illiterate. When Darrell started talking about assets, he explained how smart people understood that assets make the difference in an individual's financial stability. I was amazed at what he was saying, so I kept listening. If you have ever been a person who thought you knew something because of your many degrees, then think again. All my degrees did not prepare me for dealing with money and how to make it. There are many people out there who don't have a degree but a wealth of information on how to make money. It's pretty amazing that we allow educated people to believe that they are something "earth shattering" just because they have a degree. All they did was go to college and take advantage of the opportunities placed in front of them.

The truth is, a lot of people have not been afforded the same opportunities we have, so we can't underestimate and think that people without degrees are uneducated. In fact, most people who did not graduate from college have a different kind of education. It is called "applied knowledge," and this is the real world education that is needed for survival. So, despite my education, I was getting ready to ask a really dumb question. I knew it was coming but I could not stop myself from trying to sound intelligent in the area of finances. I said, "Well, then, why don't you all give people some of your money because you have enough to help everyone around you?" Now, I wasn't really ready for what I was about to hear, but here it goes. Darrell replied, "I tried that."

I was shocked at his answer, because many of us *other 'aires* assume that all millionaires and beyond just don't want to help others because they have been misused at one time or another by people, and so they keep their money to themselves. But Darrell taught me a very valuable lesson that I have never forgotten. For years, despite this lesson that I should have learned, I crippled some of my best and most promising students by doing things for them that they should have been doing for themselves. Darrell said, "I remember giving money to a couple who were experiencing money problems in order to help them get out of debt; but what they actually did with the money broke me down pretty badly." He had asked these people how much money they needed to get out of debt, and they gave him a dollar amount. He then gave them the money, but instead of them using the money to get out of debt, they went out and spent it on frivolous things!

I remember sitting there thinking, *If that was me I would have paid off all my debt!* Now, we can all say that with our mouths, but the truth of the matter is that when we have poverty mentalities, delayed gratification is out of the question. So, really those people are no different than us! How many times have *other 'aires* said to ourselves, "I'll pay that off with our income tax refund check?" and used that money for something else? Yeah, right! We don't pay anything off and instead use that $1,000.00 or more to go shopping, or we buy a new car that we really don't even need! Have you ever noticed that it seems for poor and middle-income people tax refund time is like a holiday? That's insane! Nowadays, there are car lots that will cash your tax return refund check for you, or even do your taxes so that you can use your refund for a new car! That's the wrong move for future millionaires! You've heard the drug ads, "Just say 'No'!"

It's astounding that we tell our kids simple things that have saved their lives and equipped them with tools that are needed for their next level. How is it that when we become adults, we think we know so much yet we know so little? It's crazy!!! Why would our kids follow us when they see very little evidence of financial stability? They look at the rappers and actresses and actors who talk about where they were going and how they got there. Contrarily, we that have poverty mentalities don't practice what we preach.

Dave Ramsey, one of my favorite financial teachers, says people should get rid of their payments! Darrell encouraged me to do the same thing, just in a different way. He said, "Own stuff. Don't rent, lease, or finance it!" I'm with Dave and Darrell, but Robert Kiyosaki believes financing can be used as leverage. I believe both Robert and Dave because they are both right. The trick is knowing if you are addicted to things that have no value.

Let me explain. My own father's vices were drug addiction, alcohol and gangsters. Research leads us to believe that if your parents had drug and alcohol problems, then you may be predisposed to the same. What they are saying is there is a great chance that you'll become addicted to drugs or alcohol if you follow the same patterns of indulgence. There is a definite truth in that, and therefore, I did not practice drinking a lot. However, between the ages of sixteen and twenty-one, I was somewhat of an alcoholic. Thank goodness, when I did turn twenty-one, I was able to quit and never go back. Hallelujah!!!

If drug and alcohol addictions can be passed down, then the same is true of poverty. The reality is that drug addiction, alcoholism and poverty can be overcome with due diligence, hard work and changing the way we think. Ignorance does not have to be an excuse that keeps us in bondage.

I believe that if you're reading this book, then you are like me and don't want to stay bound by poverty. I wasted too many years using my money unwisely. And to think, I could have been rich by now! Believe me, I am on my way because my mind-set has changed. In his book, *The Millionaire Real Estate Investor*, Gary Williams makes an awesome comment. He states that everyone will probably make a million dollars if they live long enough. He called this "the Methuselah Principle."

Have you ever pulled your credit report? Well, I pulled my wife's and mine. Over the course of six years of combined work, we had brought about $350,000.00 in our home. As I reflected on this, it made me wonder where it all went. Well, I'll tell you exactly where it went. It was spent on jewelry, clothes, cars, high-interest credit card accounts, fast food ... and other things that I cannot even account for now!!! Does this sound familiar to you? It's crazy that we blew over a third of a million dollars in six years. Now, if you average that over eighteen more years we would have made over a million dollars. Wow! I wish I would have spent it more wisely. Talk about misdirection! Please don't laugh. I bet you've done it too!!

Getting somewhere is important,
but knowing how you got there is a must...

C H A P T E R   F O U R

ONE RED BOX AND TWO STORES

ON YOUR TRIP TO BECOMING AN *other 'aire,* then you are going to have to fight for what you believe. During your journey you will feel pressure to keep up with the Joneses! Don't give in to it. Ask yourself, "Who were these people before they became the Joneses?" They were just everyday people who wanted a little bit more out of life.

I realized early on that I would have to change my mind-set in order to be successful. Living in the small town of Coffeyville, I quickly realized that I could not be a local. After all, I wanted to be a millionaire, not an *other 'aire.* At the time, I had no concept of such a thing. But in my pursuit of being a millionaire, I learned a lot. Although I am not quite a millionaire right now, the pattern for success in my life has been clearly established. Now, you may be wondering what I am talking about. The fact of the matter is that if you want to be an *other 'aire,* you must understand that success leaves a blueprint, and success for the *other 'aire* is never far away.

In this chapter, I will establish what the title phrase is all about. If you experience hard times while you are on your road to being an *other 'aire,* you will see that as long as you have a "one red box and two stores mentality," you will always find life and success in what you are doing. Back in 1999, I wanted to start a business but I wasn't quite sure what that business would be. I did not want to look for one because that would require a lot of work and I did not have time for that. So, after waiting a while, it finally happened. I should also mention to you that finding a suitable business was a process for me and it did not just manifest out of nowhere. While I was in college, in 1996, I had tried to start a business but it just never happened at that time.

NUGGET:

Don't throw away your old dreams;

they are the starting blocks of your greatness.

Now, I want you to take a minute and realize that I am not at all into wishful thinking. The Good Book says, "As a man thinketh in his heart, so is he." Early on, I had ambitions to start a clothing store, but it did not happen until the time was right for me. In fact, I came to realize that if I had not always been chasing success so much, I would have seen what was right in front of my face! We are often confronted with opportunities, but because we are not watchful and observant, they elude us. As I recall, I remember praying to God asking Him to help me open a store. I did my research, but because I didn't see it happening right away, I lost hope and let the whole thing go. I encourage you not to do as I did, and let go of your dream. Have you ever had a dream and felt like it was hopeless? Well, that is what happened to me. I quit. I felt it was not worth holding onto a dream that seemed like it would never materialize.

Some years later, while visiting my mother in St. Louis, she bought me some very nice baseball jerseys. I returned to Coffeyville with them and got such positive responses when I showed them to my friends. Now, I have always been a person who dressed nicely, long before the term "metrosexual" was ever coined. After a while, people started asking where I got my clothes and if I could get them some. I did not respond initially, because I had no idea what a gold mine this would later turn out to be. Every time I would travel, though, I would bring back some more clothing I had purchased. I became what I called an "Apparel Hunter." If people wanted certain clothing or an accessory item, I would find them and bring them back. After a while, I started having clientele come from out of the woodwork asking me about the clothing I brought back.

So much interest was generated that I asked my wife if, during our next trip to St. Louis, we could bring extra money and buy some clothing we could sell to our friends. At first she was reluctant, but eventually agreed. On our next trip I took our last $300.00 and loaded up as many clothes as I could put in a basket. My frightened wife asked if I thought I could sell that many clothes, and I told her that I didn't know for sure, but I believed I could.

NUGGET:

When you find your thing
and it feels right, do it!

Many of us are dreamers who just need a little support. These are *other 'aires* who have the ability and desire to make something out of their lives. Fortunately for me, my wife trusted that I knew what I was doing, even though I was afraid.

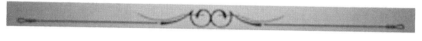

NUGGET:

Don't let fear paralyze you.
If you do it will rule you for years
and delay your increase.

Sometimes, in order to see the vision you have in your heart become a reality, you need just a little more information before you move forward and pursue it. This is not fear, but wisdom. As I've shared with you, I was determined to be successful and have my own business. On the flip side, if some of your friends and acquaintances have dreams, don't destroy their dreams, but encourage them to move forward.

After I purchased the clothes, I came back to Coffeyville and packed those clothes in a red box, which people still remember. I can't describe how excited I was during this high point of my life. The amazing thing was that I got back from St. Louis on a Sunday evening at 6:00 p.m., and by 10:00 p.m., I had sold every bit of clothing I had brought back! I even managed to make a profit in this short period of time. I was high on life because I had accomplished something and my dream had come to pass!

After the success of this small venture, I just knew I could do even more. This first experience gave me courage to step out even more. I realized that I needed another plan to accelerate growth. You see, I had only planned to succeed selling clothes out of my new red box, never imagining that I would have that much success in such a quick period of time. As an *other 'aire,* you have to make future plans. After I sold all those clothes, I prayed this prayer, "God, I don't want to peddle clothes out of a car trunk. Please bless me in finding a storefront." This is what worked for me. I had a belief, and I stuck with it.

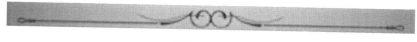

NUGGET:

*If you have a belief, then stick with it
and let it work for you.*

After praying, I did not just sit around waiting for God to miraculously drop a building out of heaven. I started looking for a building in hopes God would bless my search. It took me only two days to find the right building even though it didn't look like I could afford it. It was in the downtown mall, which in my mind was way out of my league. If you are going to be an *other 'aire,* however, you have to overcome your fears, which is exactly what I did. I called the contact number posted on the door and left a message.

On my way to work a couple of days later, I got a return call regarding that storefront space. Amazingly, it was within my price range! Everything was lining up, and I was ready and willing to pursue this new business endeavor. Without any hesitation, I responded, "I will take it!" When you have a plan and a door opens for you, you just have to walk through it! Now, some of you may be skeptical, thinking, *Are you sure you should just walk through? What happens if the outcome is bad?* Well, my response to that question is that you are not thinking like an *other 'aire*. An *other 'aire* would have already made the decision to walk through the door. Make sure you are not letting fear talk to you.

I made the decision to walk through that door and was sure glad I did! To this day, I have never regretted walking through that door. That decision was a pivotal point in my life. I am not saying that it was all easy, but at least I did it!

NUGGET:

Fear is like moat surrounding a castle:

once you conquer the moat you will

always have access to the castle.

Once you conquer fear in one area, it becomes easier to do it in other areas. The formula you used to conquer the fear the first time will be the same formula you'll use if you ever need to do it again.

Now, what's amazing is that when you make a decision to step out, people will help you. When I opened this store, all I had was a concept and a little money. That was it. After talking with a friend, Mike Souten, he asked me a powerful question that I thought I would never hear. He asked, "How much money do you need to make this happen?" I didn't even know. I had the concept and the space, but I still didn't have a true plan. I couldn't believe that I was being asked this question, so I froze up! I mean, for years I had been waiting for this dream to happen, and even though it was materializing, I still began to panic. It was a good thing he was a friend. Usually when you freeze up like that, it can kill the deal for real! My friend could see that I was speechless and scared, but he was a true friend and remained patient with me. He instructed me to think about it for a few days and get back to him with an amount.

I will never forget the feeling I got when I realized that someone wanted to fund my first project. As an *other 'aire* you will have to know where you are going. People love to help people who help themselves and are ambitious enough to pursue their dreams. I remember calling back the next day, fear in my heart. I said, "I think I can do all this with an investment of $1,500.00." "Are you sure that is enough?" he asked. "Yes," I answered, to which he replied, "Okay. I will have it to you within a couple of days." It was then that I really started freaking out! I had prayed for this to come to pass and I knew I could do it. I just had never had anyone offer financial support in this way. I was very happy, and at the same time, surprised and a little afraid. But just like he had promised, he got the money to me the next day. This story is so important to me that it inspired me to be an *other 'aire.* It represents me changing my mind-set forever!

Thanks to my friend's generosity, I opened up my first clothing store, "The Gear Box." I cannot even express how happy and proud I was! I was selling clothes and making money so fast that I was able to supplement both my wife's and my income. We were able to pocket our paychecks and utilize our overflow to purchase more items. I was on my way! I felt like the world was mine to conquer!!! After six months, our endeavor was so successful that I was nationally nominated for "Who's Who Among Businesses and Executives." I had hit a home run and I knew it. Within a year, I opened up a second shop, "The Gear Box—Phase II" with my family in St. Louis, Missouri. This store did even better than the first one! Life was great! I had a full-time job, two clothing stores, a Braid Shop, and my wife's income. It looked as if nothing could stop us. We were on the road to being rich! It was projected that both the store in Kansas and in St. Louis would gross about a half a million dollars in sales during the next year. Isn't that wonderful? This was possible because I had gotten into the clothing business just as urban hip-hop apparel was taking off in the clothing industry. There was nothing to lose! I wasn't afraid anymore. As a matter of fact, I actually got a little arrogant. People warned me that I was being prideful. I remember thinking to myself, *So what? I can do this without all the drama.* I thought they were just jealous, not knowing they were trying to tell me right from wrong.

NUGGET:

The illusion of success may
overshadow the reality of
humble beginnings.

Another lesson for an *other 'aire* is that continued success involves being able to listen, even if it hurts! But I didn't listen and that would become a hard lesson learned! Now, you're probably wondering why I am talking like this. I ended up losing everything because of my pride. I wouldn't listen. Things had started getting rough financially and I didn't care because I believed I had made it. And this wasn't the first time I felt this way.

In your journey of success, you need to watch out for pride because it will blind you. Reality was telling me that my stores were going under because I wasn't paying enough attention to them, especially in St. Louis. There was beginning to be a mess in St. Louis with the partners and I didn't do anything to stop it. Money was unaccounted for, dirty money got involved and I just overlooked it all because things appeared to be going well.

I acted like certain things were not my problem. People would ask me, "Aren't you going to do something?" I would simply ignore what was happening and figure that I had put people that I trusted in important positions whom I felt were mature enough to handle business matters. I assumed that things would just work themselves out. The biggest advice I can offer an *other 'aire* from this period of my life is to be mature and always take care of problems before they escalate. However, the right lens will put the problem in perspective.

NUGGET:

Problems seem bigger through

the wrong set of lenses.

When I failed to act in St. Louis, things began to unravel. Before I knew it, it was too late. To make matters worse, the 9/11 terrorist attack happened during this time, which affected the whole U.S. economy. Many companies suffered great losses and went under, including my own. As a result of 9/11, all of New York closed down for a week and people everywhere were too afraid to go out of their houses. This made sales drop to the bottom in both of my stores. I even shut down the Kansas store thinking that would save the St. Louis store, but it didn't. It ended up that we couldn't even pay the $1,200.00 monthly rent due in St. Louis.

Things eventually got so bad that we had to close both stores and almost eight months later, one of our partners filed bankruptcy. Just when we thought things were bad, they got worse. I started having creditors from every direction come after me. Bills totaling over $20,000.00 were accrued. Sadly, on top of all of this, I never filed as a corporation or LLC. My accountants had advised me against being one of these entities, saying that I would pay more money and double taxes. Their advice ended up hurting me even more.

In order to be successful in business, you must research the business entity that is right for you. Don't listen to people alone. Go and research the information for yourself. *Other 'aires* have this understanding because they have learned that it is better to get firsthand information than secondhand, even if the secondhand information comes from what you think is a reputable source. As a result of my not doing my own research, creditors were after me for quite some time. It would seem that I could not shake them. I had to get loans to pay back some of the debts and this made me mad! I had partners, but they didn't bother to help me out with this because they did not have the money either. Even though one partner put forth great effort, it wasn't enough financially to free us of the debt.

NUGGET:

Find partners you can trust to
help you if the going gets tough.

Eventually, by the grace of God, I did get out of debt. It was an uphill battle, and it wasn't easy. While all this was transpiring, I almost lost my wife due to physical complications with surgery and emotional strain. As an *other 'aire* you are going to have many obstacles to overcome. You have to "know your fight, fight your battle, and win the war!" You can't sit back in life and let other people make decisions for you, because if you do that, you will lose control over the outcome. I had opportunities to act and save my company, but I didn't take them.

In case you haven't realized it yet, this whole scenario is what really changed my life. Initially it changed my life for the best, but my lack of understanding also caused me to go through a lot of hardship. I learned a lot and I don't regret anything. I came to realize that I couldn't depend on anyone to save me from poverty and bad credit because it was my responsibility. When all of the money was rolling in, everyone wanted a piece of the action. When it was gone, however, no one would help.

NUGGET:

Spend most of your time with people who will build you up, not drag you down.

From this situation I realized that people with a poverty mentality are not always the best to hang around. On the other hand, business-minded people will help you if you get into a jam. Your poor friends can only be cheerleaders, they won't be able to do anything for you financially. I'm not saying dump all your poor friends. I am not an elitist. I'm just saying you need to surround yourself with people who will push you higher, while you push them higher. If your friends are not trying to be *other 'aires,* then leave them and come back later to pick them up. It is easier to carry your weight without adding their weight to your load.

My poverty streak started because I failed to react in a timely manner. The lessons I learned from my first entrepreneurial experience have left an indelible mark on me. Don't let my mistakes frighten you. When you find an opportunity to pursue your dream, you will understand the excitement I experienced. So, as an *other 'aire,* go out there and get "one red box and two stores." You deserve it! Just be watchful for pride and arrogance. They'll be waiting to trip you up if you don't keep your eyes wide open!

CHAPTER FIVE

PLAYING
WITH TOYS

THERE IS A PARTICULAR SICKNESS THAT you will have to be cured of on your journey to success. Many of us who have come from poverty backgrounds have experienced it. It involves either being denied things as a small child, or having them taken away, and it can have a devastating influence on the way you view material possessions.

I can remember being a little child and having everything my little heart desired – brand-new BMX bikes and Atari games, and living in one of the biggest houses on the block. I was fortunate enough to have these things because my father, Augusta Bond, had a very good job at Washington University in St. Louis. As a child I never really knew exactly what he did for a living, but he did make a lot of money during that time period. He was a great man, but like all men, he had his own problems. His stemmed from the fact that he was a Vietnam veteran who had been traumatized and damaged as a result of the war.

I share this information with you so that you will understand how I developed my ideas about poverty and wealth. Have you ever had the experience of everything going well in your life and then BOOM! You run smack dab into a wall? This is what happened to our family. Although financially successful, my father was abusive, and so my mother decided to remove me and my two brothers from this situation and make a go of it on her own. I would like to commend my mother for taking this step of faith on our behalf. She is a very dynamic woman and for that I owe her a debt of gratitude. Unfortunately, she had become accustomed to the lavish lifestyle we had experienced living with my father.

Part of the problem was that my mother was a proud woman who would never ask anyone for help. For many years I ascribed to this same philosophy, but over time I came to realize that my mother was wrong! She did what she thought was the best for us at the time and taught us to work hard to get what we wanted in life. Where I disagree with her is that she was prideful, which prevented other people from helping us. If you really want to change your life and finances, one of the things that has to go is pride. This doesn't mean destroying your self-worth. Pride and self-worth are two different things. The definition of pride is: "A feeling of superiority; a haughty attitude shown by somebody who believes, unjustifiably, that he or she is better than others."[1]

Now, you may be wondering how I can say this about my mother. The reason is that she raised me to be just like her. Pride has kept many poor people poor, because they believe they are too good for help. This also makes them take on certain attitudes that make it hard for people to get along with them. This is actually arrogance. Our arrogance and pride cause us to keep up a certain image costs a lot of money to maintain. My mother had us look the part because that's what we were accustomed to. But we no longer had the same income we had when we were living with my dad. As they say in the streets, we were "frontin'." My mother would lose sight of the fact that even though our dad's home was affluent, it was abusive, and she had left it to remove us from physical harm. Her decision had caused us to become poverty-stricken, but she wouldn't allow us to show it or receive help from anyone. At the time there was an old saying from a deodorant commercial, "Never let them see you sweat!" which may have been my mother's motto!

My mother really took that to heart because even though our family was struggling, no one ever knew. We hid it, from even our family members. She kept this charade going because she didn't want people to view us as trash. Although I thank my mother for doing the best she knew how to do, I believe there is a better way.

I get tired of watching poor people do what my family did. I believe they do it out of ignorance. I am talking about trying to keep up with "The Rockefellers" when you are in no position to do so. Poor people allow themselves to be victims of consumerism, when they know darn well that they can't afford to spend all the money they do. They go out and buy expensive cars like Mercedes Benzes, BMWs, Hummers, and the like, but they live in shacks and are late on all their bills. If they are not careful, all of their toys will end up in a resale toyshop called the pawnshop.

I remember when I was little child that Christmas was the most depressing time of the year for our family. A time that was happy for so many families was miserable for us. My mother tried to keep up with the Rockefellers a.k.a. the Joneses. She would go out for Christmas and buy us gold chains at $200.00 a pop, shoes, clothes, and whatever she thought we wanted, even though she could not afford it. Back then, $200.00 for gold chains was a lot of money to spend on three small boys. She, like everyone else, went out and charged up several thousand dollars worth of stuff for her children. The debt she accumulated would make her so depressed that it affected us emotionally, causing us to become resentful every Christmas. She didn't want her children to lack anything, which was noble but not realistic. She wanted to be thought of as the greatest mother alive, so she got us whatever we wanted.

As a result of this mind-set, she did not even want us to get jobs when we were in high school. Now, I realize that most parents will do whatever it takes to make sure their children don't suffer, but not all suffering is bad. It drives us to greater levels of perseverance. Not having everything handed to you is not bad either because it propels and fans the fire to be greater in life. My mother never let this happen to us, so in essence, she wound up with a bunch of spoiled rotten kids who couldn't survive without their mother. I know people now who do the same thing with their children, and in the long run, it ends up being a handicap.

My mother set the example, which was to get whatever you want and don't worry about spending the money. She even did rent-to-own – talk about a bad deal! She did not realize that sometimes by doing this, you end up paying 200 percent interest.

As I got older, I began to do like Momma did and collect my toys at any cost. I had cars, clothes and jewelry, which were always my favorites. The only problem was that I borrowed it all!!! I remembered my first encounter with credit cards was during college. When you first get into college, companies give young people credit cards like candy (and I LOVED candy!!!). What I didn't know was that you have to pay all that money back with a great amount of interest! You would think I would have learned something from watching my mother struggle. But nope! I didn't! Instead, I continued with the same behavior for years, getting hooked on the supposed "good life" that so many rappers rap about. Unlike me, however, many rappers have that kind of money to spend.

On the cover of *Rich Dad, Poor Dad,* by Robert Kiyosaki it says, "The things that rich people teach their children that poor and middle class don't." I believe what Robert speaks is the truth because I have seen this in my own behavior. The time of parents saying, "Do what I say and not what I do" is over! Children model the behaviors of their parents and environment. So be aware, if you have bad money management skills, then nine times out of ten your children will inherit them, unless you do something about it.

For many years, the toys I had were very expensive and my behavior never changed. Please understand that there is nothing wrong with toys, you just need to be able to afford them! In college, my toys started out simple, but as time went on they became very expensive! Now, you would think that having five cars at one time, a home recording studio, rental properties, land, clothing stores, and stocks would be a good thing. Well, they are, but not if you are still paying for all of them at the same time! I call them all "toys" because they were just there for the purpose of playing around, so that I could be like the chicken that laid the egg and said, "Look what I did." I am now at a point in my life where I am tired of having toys, living in poverty, and having no money saved.

So my advice to you is to decline them for now, and wait until you can afford them. Then you can play away! In the book of First Corinthians, chapter 13, verse 11, the author Paul has this to say: "When I was a child, I used to speak like a child, think like a child, reason like a child;

when I became a man, I did away with childish things" [NASB]. What I have come to realize is that I was being childish needing to have all my toys. Lately, I have been thinking, *Can I still learn as a child, instead of acting like one?* You see, we are to be like children, but that is more about having an open heart to new ideas than having a lot of expensive stuff to play with. So I no longer want the toys that I used to desire unless I can pay for them up front or comfortably.

One day, as I sat down watching the rapper Nelly on TV, I made a shocking discovery – I realized that I could have whatever Nelly had if I was willing to buy it. You see, the difference between millionaires and us is that they can go and get what they want free and clear (for the most part). Regular, everyday people have to make payments. The trick is getting lump sums of money versus making payments.

At one time, I too had diamond watches, diamond and gold customized dog tags, and rings, but after I bought all of that I was broke, busted, and disgusted. I mean, I was mad at life after I realized that I did not have any money. I later learned a term I wish I had known earlier on: "delayed gratification." This means saving up money today and waiting for tomorrow, when you can pay for what you want free and clear. Now, I have a question for you. Can you wait for what you want or do you need your toys now? Why borrow today when you can save for tomorrow and have more later? Toys are great and fun, but learn to live life by saving for them. Learn to invest your money and then you'll get to spend it later. Also, when it comes to investing you can use other people's money if you have a good business plan. Then you can develop businesses to make a profit rather than spending money on not-for-profit stuff.

I would like to share another story with you that has had a great impact on my life. During one of our family's trips to Kansas City, I met a man at a gas station who was driving a very nice toy (a Dodge Viper). I asked him what he did for a living and he answered, "I am a contractor." He then asked me, "What do you do with your money?" The way he worded his question struck me because it was very obvious that I wasn't maximizing the use of my money. He then informed me that he had another black Viper at home. I remember feeling unsettled for the rest of our trip because I could see that this man had everything I wanted out of life.

What I saw in this man was contentment and joy without worries. His warm greeting and positive attitude helped me see the futility of my own life. I could see that he had a generous spirit and was very well liked by the people in the store. As I observed his demeanor, I believe what I had that day was an encounter with divine knowledge. I have since come to understand that toys are for everyone to enjoy but when to get them is a matter of proper timing. As for myself, I decided that I would put away my toys and only get them when I could afford them. So, my advice to you is to get rid of the toys in your life until the time is right for you to have them, and then you'll be truly able to enjoy them.

[1] Encarta Dictionary Online—*World English Dictionary* Copyright 2006 Microsoft Corporation.

CHAPTER SIX

I'VE BEEN TO
THE PAWNSHOP

A PERSON CAN WORK HARD ALL of his/her life resisting stereotypes and defeating generational inheritances, only to find out that he/she have taken on the exact same behaviors he/she thought had been overcome. I want to be perfectly transparent in this book because I believe keeping secrets from you will hinder your forward progress and slow down your growth process. I want to share any relevant information for the benefit of everyone who reads this book. Please don't take this information lightly. Learn what you can from my experiences. I wouldn't want anyone to make the same mistakes I did.

As a result of my extravagant lifestyle, I had gotten into the habit of going to pawnshops (not once, not twice, but several times), and I knew it was time to stop! I'm sure many of you have been to the pawnshop too, so you can probably identify with some of the mistakes I've made. Or maybe you've had a "pawnshop experience" of sorts where you traded things of value for cash. One example is the payday loan (PDL). This is another type of pawning system in which you pawn your future paychecks (and pay a fee) for immediate cash, instead of waiting to buy things when you get the actual paycheck in your hand. All of these experiences are about using things to pay off a debt now, instead of waiting until you have the money to pay it off later. The unfortunate thing is that it creates a vicious cycle: Bad debts beget more bad debts.

Having to pawn things results from poor money management skills. It is a vicious system that victimizes the financially illiterate. No one goes to a pawnshop to trade things for the sheer fun of adventure. They generally are forced to do it out of desperation. Usually, they are in some kind of debt situation and have exhausted all other means of paying their bills. Now, if you can identify with this, you are not alone. I can personally attest to the dread of the pawnshop!

If you take a close look at the pawnshop system, it is nothing more than a form of highway robbery. When you pawn an item, you may not even get a third of your original purchase price in cash. If you had practiced good money management skills, you may have avoided the disappointment you felt as you traded your item for way less cash than it was worth.

Before I go any further, let's take a retrospective look at the behavior that may have led us down this path of destruction. For some odd reason, though we know it is not the best decision, we can't seem to stop the crazy madness of having to go to the pawnshop. We want to stop it, but it goes to our deepest, most uncontrollable urges to spend money on wasteful things. We have seen people around us who suffered and used debt for trading to pay off debt. We have seen our parents and other family members have these impulsive habits. Well, if you are tired of this like I was, join the party. You may have to use self-control and tell yourself to "just say no" to pawning things and PDLs.

I am convinced that the pawnshops and PDLs are not helping, but in fact, they are hurting people by keeping them more in debt. You have to get to the point where you realize that there are no "quick fixes." The only one that can get you out of debt is YOU. People with high debts are high risk. It is much more difficult to break down the barriers of poverty when you live check to check and operate off credit you don't even have. Many rent to own and run into walls when they try to make loans. Credit counseling services, Chapter 13s and the like will not help you out of debt. I have tried everything and have finally come to the realization that good money management and financial literacy are the only things that will get you out of debt. So, my advice to you is to quit looking for things to help get you out of debt because the time has come for you to have a paradigm shift and become an *other 'aire.*

NUGGET:

Refusing to see the truth now

will cost you much more later.

Don't rely on credit counseling or other things to get you financially free either. You are going to have to make a conscious decision to be responsible. Many of us faithful "pawn addicts" already know that if we don't change our ways, we are doomed to stay stuck in this lifestyle. Drug addicts are not the only ones who go to the pawnshops. Average Americans go as well, especially when they have poor money management skills. Pawnshops will make loans to anyone without pulling credit reports. Did you know that people keep their things in the pawnshop for over two months? The reason why they are in there for two months or more is because they don't have any money to get their stuff out of pawn. When you pawn things, you make payments on the money you owe. Look at this example below.

I pawned a keyboard worth $1,200.00. The amount received from the pawnshop as a loan was $500.00, plus a $50.00 fee. If you can't get the merchandise out in 30 days, it is another $50.00. Not to mention, when I borrowed the money, an additional $50.00 was added in fees. It looks like this:

Keyboard Value	$ 1200.00
Loan	- $ 550.00
Lost value	- $ 650.00 in value!!!

| Loan | $ 550.00 |
| I owed | $ 600.00 |

Every month I paid $50.00 more to keep the item from bring sold!!!

After five months of interest	- $ 250.00
Plus the original month's interest	- $ 50.00
I owed	- $ 300.00
Original Loan	- $ 550.00
New debt	- $ 850.00

Total lost on transaction:

Value lost	- $ 650.00
Owed	- $ 550.00 to pay off item
Original month interest	- $ 50.00
Late Payments	- $ 250.00
Total Loss -	$1,505.00

Do the math! If you look carefully, you will realize that they took me to the cleaners! On top of all of this, I still ran the risk of not getting my item back. And people experience these same things daily. Pawnshops sell your items, also get the money back they loaned you, and then some. So, there is no way you can win in this kind of transaction. Going to the pawnshop is really a sickness. I made a decision a long time ago to never return to the pawnshop. You should do the same. That's only if you want to change your position in life. The word "pawn" comes from the French language. It means "something left as security." The word "shop" means "to bring something to a place to expose for sale."

I don't know how you perceive this, but these seem to be two different meanings that contradict each other. One word means security and the other means to expose for sale. So, here's the question: How is something that is supposed to be secured or safe now exposed for sale? Well, in a nutshell, the original intent of the pawnshop was not to get items and resell them, but that is how they make a bulk of their money. Pawnshops don't really prey on people who are intelligent. However, when people are desperate and destitute, their intelligence seems to go into survival mode or fly out the window! We all know about survival. When we are in debt, it places great pressure on us and causes us to make poor choices. We've been taught that only the strong survive, but who is going to help us be strong enough to survive the pawnshop? After all, if we pawn everything, we will eventually try to buy back our own stuff! Since it's probably not paid for to begin with, now we have an even bigger problem. I have seen it before.

People pawn things that are not fully paid for in the first place, and later they're found in the pawnshop for sale. So, now the person owes the creditor and has nothing to show for the item that was sold by the pawn. The allure of the pawnshop calls to us like crack calls to a crack addict! LOL!

I recall the shameful feelings I experienced the first time I was forced to go into a pawnshop. I felt like such a failure. As I entered the store, I thought about the string of events that had led me to such a low point in my life. I had hit rock bottom; in my mind it was official, I was a terrible money manager. Hey! I know that may sound harsh, but don't try to justify it. I don't care what anyone says, you're a poor money manager if you are pawning things. But it's not an impossible situation.

The first step to getting over a problem is to acknowledge that you have one. It took me years to acknowledge that I had a problem. I denied it like every one of you reading this book has done. So, don't take as long as I did; make a decision to accept the truth about yourself. It's the beginning of your road to recovery. Besides, who would want to be known as a debt-a-holic? I began to see that I needed help, but like everyone else, I resisted the urge to ask and walked in denial. I thought to myself often, *I don't need any help. I can do it by myself.* Man, was I ever wrong. I needed help, even if I did not want to admit it, which I finally was forced to do.

After I felt embarrassed about the pawnshops, I needed to find something a little more reputable because pawnbrokers are usually synonymous with drug addicts (crack heads, if you will). I tried to find more of a dignified way of borrowing money. I started going to get PDLs, Payday Loans. I hated the very thought of going there because it once again made me realize that I was a "B.M.M.," or in other words, a Bad Money Manager. It was really very embarrassing. After all, I was somebody and I had an image to uphold. So, in order to "save face," I sent my wife. LOL! God bless her because she was willing to go. I had a hard time even going to the PDLs place. I remember my wife and I had code names for this place because we did not want people talking about us. If you have not figured it out by now, my wife and I have made some good money. However, we always would go back to bad behavior such as shopping for clothes, cars, and jewelry. You know, all the things that most of us desire.

NUGGET:

Remember, you are poor because
of your poor choices.

Needless to say, with these bad behaviors, I sank further and further into the financial abyss. I felt like I was at the point of no return. I would often asked myself, *When am I going to stop going to pawnshops and the payday loan places?*

The next thing I tried was credit counseling to educate myself on how to consolidate my debts and manage my accounts. I decided Credit Counseling Services were the way to go. After all, I had nothing to lose, or so I thought! I was wrong again! I sent all my bills to the CCS. I thought I would be moving on and getting life on the ball, but I was wrong, wrong, wrong! After I sent my stuff to the CCS, I stopped paying my bills. The agency had them, so even if I wanted to pay my bills I couldn't. I did not have them anymore. I waited and waited for months to hear back from them and they never called me back. Their response was always, "We are working on it." I trusted them to do their jobs, but I ended up getting the raw end of the deal!

After three months of bill collectors calling and threatening to report my information to credit agencies, I decided to call and demand some answers. Before then, they had just kept telling me to hold on and giving me the runaround. I finally asked to speak with a supervisor who initially informed me that they could not find me in the system. After a long and extensive search, they finally found me, but no one had even begun to work on my case! Finding myself getting angry as I listened to their lame explanations, I asked them what was I supposed to do now that I was three months or more behind on my bills? All they said was, "Sorry for the inconvenience." At that moment, I realized that no one could really help me with my debt except God!

Being the person I am, I did not give up easily. I felt forced to file bankruptcy. What I am about to tell you is a true story about potentially filing bankruptcy for personal debt. If you're going to file bankruptcy, one thing you should know is that it's a rip-off. There are different kinds of bankruptcies, but the two most common are Chapter 7 and Chapter 13. You need to know the difference. Filing a Chapter 7 eliminates all your debts except for school loans that are guaranteed and protected by governmental agencies. The Chapter 13 bankruptcy, which is also known as the "Wage Earner's Plan," watches out for this kind of bankruptcy! When I got ready to file Chapter 13, I went to a lawyer (remember, I was still in the pawnshop mentality) and I told him what I wanted to do. He discouraged me from the Chapter 13 and asked me to sit down and discuss filing a Chapter 7 instead. To my surprise, I did not have enough debt to file Chapter 7. Get this, I owed over $150,000.00 and still did not have enough debt to get out of debt! He said I would qualify for a Wage Earner's Plan or Chapter 13 bankruptcy, but he would not recommend that I go this route. He began explaining the consequences of Chapter 13 bankruptcy. I listened attentively as he explained, "You must get all of your debts consolidated and a court appointed overseer will take control of all your possessions. They will sell your stuff to recuperate as much money as possible to pay off your debtors. You will be responsible for paying off what is left in a payment plan and/or monthly installments until the debt is cleared."

All of a sudden my life flashed before my eyes. I thought of all of my possessions, jewelry, houses, and land. My mind couldn't fathom accumulating all this, only to risk it being sold. The lawyer was emphatic in his explanation. As you may have guessed, I did not like this and there was no way I was going to give up the things I had worked so hard for. Isn't it amazing how this Chapter 13 method of bankruptcy is similar to that of a pawnshop? They take your stuff to pay your debt. The lawyer offered more clarification by telling me, "In addition, if you miss a payment or two, your case will be canceled and you'll have to go through the whole process again." I said, "You mean to tell me that if I don't make payments on time, not only will I have lost everything, but I will have to start repaying money I already paid back?" He said, "Absolutely." This sounded like a catch twenty-two situation. The lawyer agreed. The reason why I was there in the first place was because I could not pay my bills on time. The next words that came out of his mouth would haunt me for years. He said that 89 percent of Chapter 13s fail.

I looked at him, puzzled, and asked, "Well, what am I supposed to do?" He did not even hesitate to give me his recommendation. He informed me of his belief that most people who file Chapter 13 fail in the process of completion. Chapter 7 was the next option, but in order to qualify I had to buy some more things on credit. This cycle is madness. I politely said, "Thank you" and told him to bill me as I left, laughing hysterically.

NUGGET:

Debt is like a boa constrictor –

the more you resist dealing with it,

the tighter it squeezes.

I realized that debt begets debt. The only thing that will change it is the right mentality toward capital producing ventures. It's like that age-old saying, "I can do bad all by myself." Going to the pawnshop did not cause all of this, but it did push me to the edge of the debt abyss. If you want to win over this cycle, debt has to end! There are only a couple of ways to get rid of debts. You must focus your energy on paying bills on time and saving money to eliminate debt. You must also create a vacuum by developing ingenious opportunities that will generate large amounts of funds to cover and suck up a bulk of debt at one time. (I'll explain this in greater detail later on.)

The root of all debt is the mind-set of a person. If a person only knows poverty, then he will reproduce what he has known, unless that mind-set is broken. Most books do not address the power of poverty, but I assure you that it is real. I remember being in a graduate class and Dr. Richard Lipka gave an enlightening presentation about S.E.S. – socioeconomic status. In brief, this simply means that low-income people lack the resources that middle and upper class people have, and seem to be stuck at this level of life according to their S.E.S. factor. Poverty is a way of life and encompasses a mentality that must be broken.

In order to fix a pawnshop mentality, a person must educate and equip himself with financial literacy. This will then equip that person with sound judgment about personal economics. I am not saying I am a psychologist, but rather that I was a victim of my own financial ignorance. Experience is the best teacher. The *other 'aire* method offers education that will be instrumental in enabling a person to see opportunities as they come their way. When you are in survival mode, a.k.a. "pawnshop mentality," you miss opportunities. In order to help your situation, let's think a few minutes and ponder on our past mistakes. You know what they are. That's why I am encouraging you to take a good hard look at and correct your mistakes. If you need assistance, find an accountant. That's exactly what I did, and it was worth every cent. A bookkeeper can be a good weapon in your arsenal. In the book *Rich Dad, Poor Dad*, Robert Kiyosaki writes about having a team made of financial advisors, accountants, lawyers, investment consultants, etc.

Getting an accountant was the best thing I ever did, and I try to encourage others to do the same. On average, the accountant fees ranged from twenty-five to fifty dollars a month. It may seem like a lot at first, but it's not compared to overdraft charges, fees, late fees, and all the financial charges you will end up paying by doing it yourself. With finances, it is not always a good idea to be a "do it yourself" person. An accountant will guard your money from your number one financial enemy: you. I'm not joking. When you've lived with a poverty mentality, you need to be trained, and an accountant can help start this process immediately. Today, if you are reading this book, make your decision to come and stand with me like many others. When you meet me in the near future, I want you to come up to me and say, "I've been to the pawnshop" as a sign that you're not going there anymore. Realize you're greater than the debt you are in! Shake the dust off your feet and move on quickly! Don't think about what you're going to do, just do it.

I have come up with several methods to avoid the pawnshops which I am sharing with you here.

1. Don't be a pawn to poverty. Have you ever played chess before? While I will be using the word "pawn" in a different way, it still captures the way we act in a pawnshop mentality. Remember this to help yourself.

2. Be a MVP (most valuable piece). In the game of chess, a pawn is one of the least valuable pieces. It only has the power to move forward (one square at a time), to move to a square diagonally forward, and to be promoted to any other position piece except for the king, upon reaching the eighth rank. What I'm saying is that a pawn can only move one step at a time. You may have thought you were making forward steps by going to the pawnshop, but my math illustration shows you that you are really taking one step backward when you walk into one of those places. And remember, a pawn cannot be a king. Therefore a pawn has no real ability to gain: no king, no millionaire, no C.E.O., no president, no ability to rule, not even over your own stuff! Remember the Chapter 13? I am fully persuaded that I don't want to be a pawn anymore.

3. Know your position. Be disciplined and stay away from pawnshops, PDLs, and anything like them. Proper positioning is very important; it simply means you will never ever be a king with a pawn mentality.

Once the storm is over,
you must prepare for the flood...

CHAPTER SEVEN

BELOW ZERO

IN THIS DAY AND AGE, BEING poor doesn't seem so uncommon. However, if you were to ask people if this was their goal in life they would emphatically say, "NO!" There is no glory in being poor. It is not fun. No matter how much people tell their stories about the "good ol' days" and how far they used to walk to school barefoot in the snow, I cannot imagine that there was any fun in that type of life. Older people tell these types of stories to younger generations for the purpose of making us take heed to them. So, for the purposes of this book, let's set the record straight: Poverty is no fun. It never was, and it never will be, no matter how touching your grandfather's story is. There's nothing great about being in a state of poverty where your needs are not met. Everyone wants their needs met. That doesn't necessarily mean they want to be rich. In my opinion, people just want to live a comfortable life.

I've entitled this chapter "Below Zero." Have you ever felt less than zero? Chances are, if your attitude made you feel like that, you probably felt less than zero long before then. Most people haven't realized that how far a person goes in life depends upon their attitude. You have to make up your mind that you are "somebody" and then live your life in that manner. You need to make a choice to be better than zero. For the record, let's just say you feel less than zero. You will have to adjust your mind-set because this thinking will discourage you, causing you not to try harder to accomplish better things for yourself. You need to find out what your good assets are and think on them. Feeling less than zero can distort your perception of the state of poverty you truly are in.

Before we continue, however, I have a couple of questions for you:

1. If you were worth any amount of money, how much would it be?

2. Did you know that in society's eyes you are worth something?

Get ready to find out that you are truly worth something and that you will actually be able to calculate your own value after this.

What most of you will come to realize is that you are worth less than zero. You will understand that in our economic system, everyone has a numeric value. There are truly people below zero in the eyes of society according to financial statements. Financial worth is an accumulation of your debts and assets balanced to figure out what we call your "net worth." It's true, most of us are worth less than zero. I was shocked when I found out my value to society. You too will be shocked after you find out your worth, whether it is good or bad. Being below zero is a drag and you're not going to want to stay there long. Poverty is no picnic.

The first time I found out I was worth less than zero, I was about twenty-seven years old. I was trying to get loans and every time I applied, the banks kept turning me down. If a bank has ever turned you down, you are not going to want to miss this. When I went for these loans, I was always unprepared and never had my act together. The first question the bank would usually ask was, "Do you have any collateral?" Of course, not knowing what collateral was, I would ask, "What is that?" They would inform me that they needed something of value from me to hold on to in exchange for the money that they were going to loan me. Let me repeat that collateral is an asset you can offer as leverage in the loan process. In layman's terms, you need something of value that the bank will hold, like a deed or title to land in exchange for cash.

Even after I learned what collateral was, it still took a long time for me to get a loan because at the time I didn't own anything, not even a car. If you are financing a car, let me tell you the truth right now, you do not own it, even though you may think you do. I repeat: You do not own it. You see, you may tell all your friends about your new car, but until you pay for it completely, the lender or the bank still owns it. You only have what is called a "vested interest" in it. Vested interest means that you own a percentage in the thing you purchased. I recall thinking I owned my van that was financed, but I really didn't own it. I just thought

I did. I didn't own it free and clear. So, I could not use it for a loan unless my vested interest was great.

NUGGET:

If you owe it, you don't own it.

If you have enough equity or vested interest in something like a car, you can borrow money on it; but you have to have a great amount invested, and usually with good credit.

Here's an example of equity or vested interest:

The value of your car	$ 5,000.00
You still owe	<u>$ 2,000.00</u>
Equity/Vested Interest	$ 3,000.00

By this example, you could borrow $3,000.00 in cash because you now have equity in an asset. However, most people will only deal with equity in a house. Home equity usually has bigger numbers to deal with. Banks are more apt to loan money on home equity versus equity in a car. If you have a good rapport with a small local bank, that can help you get a loan.

Now, I'm warning you right now that when you go to the bank, please beware because it may make you angry. I was not adequately prepared prior to going to the bank. I did not know the difference between net worth and debt-to-income ratio. Debt-to-income ratio is the amount of your monthly income less your monthly debt. The amount of money left is assigned a percentage. When you have high debt, your income has less value to the banks. Banks generally want you to have 45 percent to 50 percent of your income left open before they will loan you any money. Now keep in mind, when I explain net worth, you will also get an understanding of another term: financial statement. Net worth is the total amount of your assets, less your liabilities. Net worth is factored up by filling out a financial statement – a mathematical application to calculate one's value.

Robert Kiyosaki defines an asset as anything that brings you money. For example, a rental home, your home, boarding room/rent or business are assets. If you get money from some type of stocks and bonds, retirement IRAs, or anything like these, then you have assets. So, here is a mathematical example:

Assets (Paid in full)

Owned Cars	$ 5,000.00
Owned house rental	$ 50,000.00
Stocks	$ 40,000.00

Retirement IRA	$ 30,000.00
Total	$125,000.00

Liabilities

Personal house	$ 75,000.00
Credit cards	$ 2,000.00
Totals	$ 77,000.00

After taking assets of $125,000.00, minus debt of $77,000.00 = $48,000.00. Now you can understand that your net worth is $48,000.00. I did this very simple math problem so you can get an idea of how much you're worth. Even though I made this one positive, most of the time it comes out negative. This is because there are usually far more debts or liabilities than assets.

Let me say this, if you're going to make it in life you are going to have to ask questions. Asking questions causes everyone to grow. If you don't ask questions, you may not get the answers you need or the results that come with them. I learned how to ask questions when I went to the university. If you did not ask questions, you would not get helpful answers. Everyone can ask questions but they may not gain the answers they need to be successful. When I was in class other people asked questions, but very seldom were they my questions. The reason I suggested you learn to ask questions is because your questions may also turn the light on for someone else. Everyone learns differently and you are no exception to the rule. I encourage you to ask lots of questions when you go to the bank, too. I mean, play dumb and let them explain stuff to you like you are five years old. Believe me, it will make a world of difference.

While we are on this subject, I will share one of my secrets with you. When I want information, I have a way of collecting it. First, I have learned to never show up at anyplace in person until I have my act together. For the most part, I usually call places to get information. Now you may wonder, "Why?" The reason is because when you go to the place you called, you can be whoever you want to be and they will never know that it was you on the phone. I have been known to change my voice, my name, and even use other people to help me get the results and answers I need. What this actually does is prepare me to go in person. After I learn something, I can sound like I understand what I'm doing and talking about. I had to learn this because when you are below zero, you have to find a way to get above zero. I know that my answers lie in banks and other financial institutions because they're the ones who loan money. However, it was still amazing to me to find out that, according to their computations, I was worthless. Make no mistake about it – it is all about making money for banks. It's not about helping people, unless of course it is Community State Bank in Coffeyville, Kansas (Plug!).

As you keep reading the word "worthless" in this chapter, know that I am not degrading you, but using a little reality therapy. The word "worthless" is made up of two words: "worth" and "less." The word "worth" means to have a measurement of value. For example, one should know that diamonds and gold have high financial worth. The word "less" means consisting of a more limited amount of something. In short, it too is a word of measurement. The word "worthless" has to always be used in its proper context to grasp its true meaning. This is definitely necessary in terms of making comparisons. A 1986 Ford Ranger has a worth that's less than the value of a 2008 Mercedes CLK. Therefore, in comparison, I was worth less than people with good credit and a good job. Stability was and is a bank's highest priority. I am amazed to this day by the implications.

★ ★ ★ ★ POWER THOUGHT ★ ★ ★ ★

Transition is what you make it,
so make it work...

CHAPTER EIGHT

COMING FROM BELOW ZERO

I ONCE SPOKE TO A GROUP of mentees about money management. When I first started dealing with the fact that the majority of Americans are worth below zero, people resisted what I was saying because no one wants to feel like a fool. I know when I accumulated all my things, I thought they would make me happy, but I was wrong. I now realize that people don't like to hear about being below zero because it says two things about them. 1. Ignorance is spending all your hard-earned money on things of no true value. 2. Financial literacy needs to be a top priority. Many people get between a rock and a hard place, and into situations they are too ashamed to admit. I found that most people don't want to look or feel stupid because it leads to feelings of helplessness.

Now, we cannot proceed any further in our study until I straighten one thing out for everyone reading. Hear me! You are not handicapped or stupid. Don't even let those thoughts enter your mind. Resist the very thought of being below zero in society's eyes. What I have learned is that if you're going to reveal a truth that is negative, then you better give some positive insight on how to move from the negative to the positive. Many people write books that tell the bad and don't really give a plan for change or improvement. This chapter will focus on "coming from below zero." If you have been to the pawnshop and are below zero, then now is the time to turn things around. As

COMING FROM BELOW ZERO

an *other 'aire,* you already have the ability in you to change your situation. You have just been ignoring it. I am getting ready to give you a blueprint for success so that you can come up from below zero.

To get from below zero, you need to be extreme in your efforts. If you're not serious about being an *other 'aire,* stop right here and don't go any further. The first thing you need to do is count up the cost for staying where you are. I mean, how badly do you want financial freedom? I'm not going to mislead you; it is definitely going to cost you something. You may not have a lot discretionary money for a few months or years, as you get yourself out of debt. If you want to be free, you must stop spending money on so-called luxury items like gold, jewelry, clothes, cars, etc., and all the other trappings of falsified success. Many people spend a lot of time looking like they are rich, but in reality, they are more broke than a tempered pane-glass window that has been shot out with a pellet gun. People like to have the appearance of money. But often they cannot actually say they own what they have, because it has been obtained by credit and nothing is paid for free and clear.

Look, I don't care how badly you want something. Don't buy anything unless it is for your immediate survival. Stop spending money. You may not like what I am about to say, but you need Jesus! LOL! When people say you need Jesus, what they're really saying is that you have some behaviors that you need help with. Sometimes it is beyond your natural control. I'm not trying to sell religion, but you may need a relationship with a source of personal strength that will help you focus and overcome barriers that are preventing your success. I am not necessarily talking religion, but I am simply saying "get yourself some help." If you can't manage your finances, you need an accountant. You must be willing to admit you have no discipline. An accountant will help you get that. Once you get the accountant, stay with them until you are completely out of debt. I started with an accountant and left them because my wife wanted us to get back control of our money. The truth is, we never lost control of it. She just thought we did because someone else issued our finances and told us what to do with them.

Don't go to an accountant and not take responsibility for your bills, or just give your checkbook away for no reason. It's simpler to just go give them your checkbook and have them write you a budget. However, you must live by that budget until you are financially free and not a moment sooner. Giving them your checkbook doesn't mean you give them total control because you will still sign and monitor your checks. When I have told people to do this in the past, they would always reply, "I can't do that because I am not rich." I would laugh at them and ask this question. "If you are paying overdraft charges or late fees, then how can you afford not to do it?"

Now, I repeat, don't be dumb. Don't sign anything over completely; just give them the authority to fill out your checks to pay creditors. No one should sign anything for you. All they're doing is balancing your books, bills, and managing your money. If you're like my wife and me, it is not that we didn't have the money. We just stayed broke because we did not manage our time well enough to do our books. Most people get into more debt because they don't pay their bills on time or they don't really have the money. Or they have the money but they spend it frivolously. The accountant will monitor finances carefully and get you out of debt, but you have to let go of your pride.

Next, you need to develop a savings account. As the accountant works on eliminating debt, funds should be placed in a savings account creating a snowball effect. The snowball method is nothing new. In fact, it has been around for years. This method is talked about in a lot of books, but I will give you an example of it. My accountant even uses it because it is a good, solid way to eliminate debt. Snowball effect is simply eliminating one bill at a time and then transferring the freed-up money to the balance of another bill. This money is transferred to another bill, and this process continues until all bills are eliminated. Begin by paying off little bills first. This gives you a sense of accomplishment. If you intend to pay the big bills first, you will eventually give up. This is what led us to getting an accountant.

Being an *other 'aire* does not allow failure to be an option, but rather a stepping-stone to success. Most people tell you not to make mistakes or fail, but failing is how we learn. The word "fail" is a verb, so there is action attached to it. So, if "fail" is a verb, then how do people use it to describe other people? Also, if "fail" is a verb, which is an action, then actions can be stopped. We have the power to stop this action and change to a new course, like success.

NUGGET:

"Fail" is a verb; therefore you cannot be a failure.

Just switch your actions from failure to success.

My personal quote states: *"Failure is not an option, but it is a must. Failure teaches us to learn from our shortcomings."* People place a great responsibility on themselves by saying that they are failures. Failing is not bad.

It is only terminal when we stay down after failing. I hope you opt out of the depressing mind-set that comes along with failure and embrace it with exhilarating thoughts of success.

After you've got your finances under control, you must know what you can invest in. The savings that you have been implementing will be very instrumental at this stage. You will need to research stocks, real estate, and other business ventures. One stream of income will very seldom make a person rich or well off. In fact, if all you want to do is retire, then you can get that from a job. If you want to be financially free, it will take research and time. Watch out for get rich quick schemes because they are out there waiting for some vulnerable, unsuspecting, and/or uneducated person.

After having spoken with various rich people, I found out that they only have these things in common: drive, keeping their word, and real estate. They all had drive. It was what pushed them to get things done. They kept their word. Oh! Wait! I'm not saying they're good people. I mean they kept their word to lending institutions and creditors. Last but not least was real estate. Almost every rich person owns real estate. The rich own real estate because it is the only real asset that can bring complete financial freedom, if it is used right. You're going to have to learn how to invest in something and it should be something you can monitor.

You need to find a stockbroker or real estate investor and learn from them. I had to learn everything I know by asking questions. I'm not joking. I wrote this book so you can get out of debt and I plan to help you on a personal level as well. I'll talk more about this help later. Continue reading, so that you are ready and equipped to come from below zero. I don't claim to be a rich man in the traditional sense, but back in the ol' days people knew how to survive. My grandmother, Elnora, is an *other 'aire* because she always has money. If anyone needed anything, grandmother could get it because her credit was great, plus she saved. I guess I didn't follow the practicality of financial literacy from my grandmother, although I should have. Elnora used to work a lot and save money and had great credit. For the record, credit is not bad, if you have discipline. My grandmother never abused her credit because she came from a time when people did not really use credit a lot, but they still had access to it when they needed it.

In our society today, credit is big business, according to Dave Ramsey. I definitely agree with him. If you look at how high interest rates are, it should cause you to wonder why very quickly. Did you know that creditors make money off you borrowing money, and then some? Listen, they're not just making money off what you borrow, they're getting a whole lot of extra money. So, we pay high interest rates on money that has never been made. Listen, when you buy a house, the bank you borrowed money from never even sends money to another bank, in most cases. They are giving you accounts to pay on (interest money) that never actually changes hands. So, you will, in essence ,pay interest on a house that you don't really own in hopes that one day you will. If you don't believe me, look on your mortgage statement. Consequently, by the time you pay your home off, you will have paid enough money to buy two homes. So, what are you going to do about it? You can keep being ignorant or change your mind-set and your behavior.

NUGGET:

It is hard to see daylight from inside a tunnel.

In the words of Stephen Spielberg's screen play, *The Color Purple,* "I know what it is like, Mrs. Celie. You want to go somewhere, but you can't." Well, guess what? You can now go somewhere because you have things to work with to free you up. So, for the record, let's recap the steps.

1. Eliminate debt by obtaining an accountant and then using the snowball effect.

2. Create a savings account that will make you feel like a million bucks, but empower you to become an *other 'aire.*

3. Invest. This will give you options for attaining wealth.

I learned something from a wealthy gentleman in Pittsburg, Kansas, named Mike. I asked, "What kinds of people should I be around if I want to be rich?" I will never forget his answer. He said, "I generally break people down into three different categories. I rate them: A, B, and C types of people." I asked, "What?" I can remember thinking that this guy is full of himself. He could see that I was looking crazy so he began to explain. "C-type people are those who talk about other people. They gossip, start confusion, and never do anything productive in life. B-type people build their lives around having things and are a little better than C-types of people. Type A people are those who build their lives on ideals, visions, and goals. These are people who are going to go somewhere in life." Once I heard that, I wanted to be an A-type of person, but I failed miserably over and over again. I am writing this book so you can have a smoother path to success. It is hard trying to stay in the A group if everyone around you is a B or C type of person. Besides, I did not know any A-type people at all. I needed a connection overhaul quickly.

A connection overhaul is needed when you're trying to come from below zero. You need people who think like you around you all the time. A quick look at the 2008 presidential race should help you to understand everyone has to have people around them that think like they do. For President elect Barack Obama, this was especially true when he had to distance himself from his longtime church leader because they did not see eye to eye anymore. The similar interest hindered the flow of the electoral process for the presidency because he could not work his own agenda. One may think that I went on a tangent, but I didn't. You must realize that the type of people you connect with must have the same level of thinking that you have, or they can create a disaster for you going forward.

NUGGET:

If Uncle Bubba is a thief, don't take him to your CEO's house party.

That may sound arrogant to you. However, it is a must that you take my word on this or you will definitely be sorry. Mike also enlightened me by sharing that you can't take everyone everywhere with you. They may not be ready for where you are going. Also, everyone may not be able to handle what you will say to them. It will be like a foreign language. Besides, while they are talking about other people and/or focused on buying materialistic stuff, they will not be paying any attention to your direction, even if you involve them. Oh, you can help B and C types of people. Contrarily, what I found to be true is that B and C types of people lack the ability to have delayed gratification.

I never wanted to change my friends, but if you recall earlier in the book, I said that the Walker brothers asked me how long I was going to be "ghetto." If you are from a background of poverty, you'll understand what I am saying because it is hard to change from a poverty mentality. I am neither arrogant nor conceited. The truth is that I did not want to leave my friends for a long time. What I learned over time is that if you do have a drive to go somewhere, you can't always take your friends with you.

So, another way of coming from below zero is disconnecting from some people and connecting with others. You may need a connection overhaul. Don't waste any more time doing things that won't profit you. Overhaul your life. If you want to be an *other 'aire* badly enough, you will make a change. I'm convinced that you'll understand how to come from below zero because the formula is easy, but it takes commitment.

NUGGET:

No press, no success.

Please don't waste an *other 'aire* minute. Upgrade your financial management and your friends. Here is a secret that is not for the weak-minded. There's a quick and easy way to get out of debt and it is the only true vacuum for quick debt elimination. Your house is your only true way of getting out of debt, but most people won't want to do what I'm about to suggest. This is not new, but if you have ever known of anyone that foreclosed or filed bankruptcy, chances are they had to do this. Your house, if it has equity in it, is your way out. Stop before you take out a home equity loan or a second mortgage. Stop! Refinancing to get out of debt is often encouraged. What people don't realize is that you are not getting out of debt when you go that route. You're just transferring debt. Most of the time, people get upside down in their house and never get it paid off. Upside down in your mortgage means that you owe more than your house is worth.

So, here's the plan. Sell your house if it has enough equity to pay off your debts. This may sound devastating and drastic because then you won't have a house, but you will be back to zero to have a fresh start. Another thing is that you will be much wiser. However, I am not pushing this, given the state of the economy. (I told you it was not for the weak-minded.) Your house will suck up all your debt like a vacuum and then you'll have no more debt. Then buy an old house and not a new one. Try to find a fixer-upper, and then eventually move out of it and use it for rental property. Now, after you have that rental property and it is generating income, go buy your house or keep this same method going until you have enough money to buy a house outright. Wouldn't that be great? You can do this in about five short years. The benefit is that you now have collateral, which is known as leverage, and you are making money. Not bad for selling your house five years ago. Now you have access to start building wealth for your future. See, you are definitely becoming an *other 'aire.*

Don't hold back. All you can do is fail. Contrary to what people believe, failure is great if you can learn from it. The Good Book says that a righteous man will fall seven times, but he will get back up. This excites me because it is an option in the form of making mistakes. Abraham Lincoln had over ten documented failed attempts at pursuing his goals, but he did not give up and neither should you. There is a new slogan to adopt, "Failure is more than an option; it is an opportunity." Not being afraid to fail will keep you trying. The day you stop trying is when you truly fail. I know I've already said similar things, but I will keep repeating these concepts until your brain is saturated with new understanding. It's only when you quit that you truly become a failure and not a moment before. So, I encourage you to fail.

In the Good Book, there is a story about a wealthy man who left his three stewards with some money. Each had a responsibility to do something with the money he had given them while their master was away. The first two invested and earned a return, but the third one hid his portion in the ground. Upon return, the master asked each of his servants what they had done with the money. The two who had invested it replied, "We invested your money and made more money." The one who buried the money confessed to his master what he had done. He claimed he did it because he knew his master was a hard man. Well, guess what? That made the master mad, because this last servant had played it safe with his master's money. My point is that if we are afraid to make mistakes due to the possibility of failure, we lose out on a great opportunity of gain due to fear.

In today's society, we've been conditioned not to try. That's why people keep playing life safe and lose heart in changing their situation. I've failed many times, but I don't consider myself a failure. Every successful person in the world has had some level of failure. I'm certain if you had a chance to ask them, they would tell you that their setbacks and failures are what made them great. I realize that coming from below zero is not easy, but if you want it badly enough, you will risk failing ten times because you know that the end result will be sweeter than never trying.

Don't let any negative factors keep you from coming from zero and experiencing your ultimate success.

★ ★ ★ ★ **POWER THOUGHT** ★ ★ ★ ★

Don't stay at zero
when ONE is just a step away...

CHAPTER NINE

STAYING OUT OF REHABILITATION

WHAT I AM ABOUT TO SHARE with you may seem odd because it sounds crazy. Once you are above zero and everything is straightened out in your life (financially and mentally), you'll have to fight staying away from your drugs. Debt and bad money management are addictive and require a means of rehabilitation. If you are really committed to staying clean, it is going to be a fight. I remember when I went to my accountant for the first time. I did not like it, but it was necessary for me to turn over my personal financial management control. I kept control of authorization of funding but my accountant had the power to do what was needed to get me out of debt. Initially, it was a little easier to get things done because my wife and I owned a clothing store and hair braiding shop. We turned over our employment income paychecks to living mainly off of the profits of our investment. We survived. The amazing thing is that in one year our accountant was able to eliminate over $16,000.00 of our debt. It's simply because, as I mentioned in the previous chapters, she used the snowball effect. I was amazed at how fast timely payments eliminated debt.

Contrarily, after she got us out of debt, it only took about six months for us to need help again. LOL! Just like drug addicts, we went right back to poor spending habits, and that time on even crazier things and bigger expenses. It was after six months of being clean and sober that I thought I was free from what had trapped me. The reality is that even if people get out of debt, they will still go right back to their old habits. This is called a "conditioned response." Years ago, I learned in psychology about tests that were performed on a lab rat. In this experiment, they put a rat in a cage and electrified the floor. First, the rat just ran around the cage, but when they would shock the floor of the cage, the rat would run around until it found safety. This safety was a small piece of the floor that was not shocked. In this experiment, eventually the rat knew that the shock would come on the floor. So after a while, it no longer wanted to be freed or run around. In fact, it just gave up. The rat became conditioned to its environment and felt no need to be brave. It returned to a safe corner that did not receive the shock. Even when food was put in the opposite corner to see if the rat would move, the rat stayed in its comfort zone until it eventually died.

I have experienced similar situations. Due to the shock of my environment, I lost my ambition and drive. Some of you reading this book may have a similar mind-set. I've tried and tried to get out of debt and it never seemed to work. Most people, like this rat, will give up and eventually die. If you take a drug addict or alcoholic and ask them why they partook in bad habits, they will say because they need them to feel good or to survive. They also say it takes all the pain away. They will say that it helps them cope. Sometimes, after a drug addict or alcoholic has spent years of focusing on being clean, they will return to what is safe and familiar. I know you may be asking, "How can that be safe?" Well, let's take a prisoner who has been in jail for ten years. Once he is released, he goes back to what he used to do prior to incarceration, so he can go back to the "safety" of prison. There are some prisoners who won't call anyone outside of the prison because they're afraid of change. Similarly, even though we are outside of the jail, we think it is dumb to want to stay in jail. To a prisoner of ten years, it's not. Just like the rat, there seems to be no more hope. Although these prisoners' visions and dreams for life seem to be gone, the real truth is that they're lying dormant waiting for an opportunity to be revitalized. So, actually, everything is still in place. The mind has just accepted the conditions of its present circumstances as being permanent.

However, if someone could convey to the rat, the drug addict, the alcoholic, the prisoner, and the person in bondage to debt, that all is not lost, then the zest for life would be reignited in them. It is often said that a person's perception is their true reality. In other words, if someone believes that they're doomed to stay in a certain condition or reality, they are pretty much trapped in that mentality. This was true for me. I thought it would be way too hard to get out of debt. I even thought since I was halfway out of debt, I could spend money because I was doomed to stay in debt. I accepted this reality because it was taking too long to get out of debt.

NUGGET:

Never rush progress. Like quicksand,
the faster you move the deeper you sink.

I was tired of waiting for the final day of relief. That day seemed like it would never come and as long as I thought like that it never would. Have you ever noticed that when you get impatient about something happening, it almost seems like it will never come? That day never seemed to come for me until I became an investor and started collecting assets instead of liabilities. I just had to shift my perspective. But I will warn you. It was hard changing my behavior. It was even harder to change my mentality. Needless to say, change is essential if you want to be free. I changed my bad habits, stopped needless shopping frenzies, and became determined that I would not stay in that state.

Listen, I believe in you and you should believe in yourself. What I am saying, in short, is that a person has to believe they can be free. If they don't, they are powerless to change their situation and they will stay in that same place. This book is indirectly getting you to have a paradigm shift. If you shift your mind-set, you will know that nothing is impossible. Rehabilitation is one important key to being an *other 'aire*. *Other 'aires* fall off just like billionaires and millionaires. The difference is that the *other 'aire* usually fails/falls without a safety net. However, even though they are broken, they will still emerge from the failure. *Other 'aires* know that they must constantly monitor their behavior and mood swings.

In earlier paragraphs, I metaphorically placed bad debt in the some category as drugs. Rehabilitation is part of the process of making a new start. However, you don't want to constantly return to rehab. Most people do not realize that spending money and accumulating debt are symptoms of the same sickness. Spending money is a sickness when you don't have it. Not having things is what causes people to spend money. This sickness works in two ways. The first way is that of a person who didn't have anything growing up. They tend to spend more money trying to compensate for the things they did not have when they were little. I don't believe that I am alone in this thinking. If you turn on a TV station that deals with new moneymakers, they will often mention it. They will say that they were deprived of name-brand items and couldn't afford shoes like Nikes. So, when they do get money, they are relentless and buy six pairs every time they go shopping. Even though they can afford it, this spending actually creates problems for the youth in today's society. Young people are watching this and develop a fake reality of what true wealth is. They will go out and buy the high priced stuff that their favorite celebrity has. Sometimes this false reality contributes to young people going out and doing illegal things for material gain. So, I don't believe that I am the only one who has done this. It doesn't take a rocket scientist to see what is right in front of your face.

The other side of this coin is that people who did not have a lot growing up can be really cheap and overly conservative. They just hoard money, and this does not include saving or investing. Most of the time, they're not in the conserving mode; they are in a fearful mode, believing they could lose what they have any minute.

What they don't realize is that money will disappear, even if they don't spend it. If they just live off of it, their living expenses will eventually consume what they've hoarded over a period of time. Neither one of these extremes is good because they both are based on fear. It actually shows how they are afraid of life. People who are deprived usually don't admit that they have a problem with finances. Instead, they continue with this behavior. Isn't it interesting that the majority of people who grew up with nothing usually stay poor? You can't just wish poverty or being lower or middle class away. One has to work, be smart and change one's way of thinking to get out of this way of life.

I used to think that I had to have the most expensive things in the world. I would buy purses for my wife ranging from $265.00 for a Dooney & Burke to $700.00 for a Louis Vuitton. I thought nothing of spending $600.00 to $1700.00 for an Omega Seamaster watch. I needed all these things so that I could shed the signs of poverty, and all the while I still had a poverty mentality inside.

Reality check! Hello! I remember Eddie Murphy said something in a standup comedy routine many years ago that stuck with me. He said, "Nothing from nothing leaves nothing." If you're poor, then looking wealthy will not change the facts of that reality. If you have nothing and you are buying stuff, then buying stuff will leave you with less than nothing. Again, nothing leaves nothing. So, your things will end up being sold or taken away. This is why you want to stay out of rehab. You should be taking steps forward. Returning to rehab means you're going backwards. It means that those ol' bad habits are returning for a second life. Don't give in to those urges. Please, put on the brakes and stop. You don't want to keep going backwards.

I'm amazed when I see celebrities come out of and go back into rehab. You may ask yourself, "Why aren't they just happy with their lives? I mean, they have so much money." Even though the "bling" looks good, make no mistake about it, money is definitely not the cure-all-be-all we've been led to believe. This will be a good place to stress, once again, that money isn't happiness. It can only help provide a means to happiness.

Often as I watch the news, I notice the same people going in and out of rehab. Rehab signifies that there is a recurring problem in someone's life. After all, the word is "re-habilitation." This word "habilitation" is something being built. The prefix "re-" means again. So there is a building or developing going on again. If they are back, then something didn't get taken care of completely the first time, or else this person would not need more help in what was already being offered.

I hope you are coming to see that I am offering you serious help in this book. But I cannot apply it for you; that's up to you. Please don't go back to rehab because it means you went backwards, and you should always be moving forward. Even though I have slipped back a few times myself, I now know that I am out for good. I know because the things I have learned and experienced have made lasting changes in me. Don't be afraid to change, especially your mind-set. Stay clean, and stay out of rehab.

The detail of your reality
is truth waiting to happen…

CHAPER TEN

ASSESSING
THE TRUTH

AFTER RUNNING YOUR COURSE, YOU SHOULD now be realizing that you have to make changes in the way you think or your life will be spent grasping at air. You may end up wasting time and living in an old shack. This book really only asks one question, which is, "How badly do you want it?" Do you really want it badly enough to do whatever it takes to change your thinking and your life? You see, I've taken you through the pages of this book for the purpose of giving you the greatest treasure I have found. I believe, like me, you will love it more than millions of dollars.

I remember listening to an older woman whose words of wisdom shined a little light upon my life and exposed it to some serious truth. This woman began by talking about her life and how she had previously made seven figures a year in sales. As you can imagine, I was all ears, listening attentively and waiting to hear what she had to say next. I sat in awe, anticipating every word that would come out of her mouth. She first started by talking about her business, but soon after that, she started talking about her life. Now you have to know me in order to visualize how my face may have looked when she changed the subject. I like for people to talk about the same subject rather than switch to an "other." Nevertheless, I made myself listen to what s he was saying. I have to admit though, that thought that popped into my mind was, *Okay, do I really want to hear this woman talk about her life?* Well, I was immediately reminded that sometimes we need to be quiet and let God talk to us the way He wants to – to just be quiet and listen for a second. You see, God was speaking through this woman. As I listened, I wondered why this woman was not excited about me wanting to make a lot of money like she did. This lady kept on as if she did not care about the money. I was thinking in my mind, *She doesn't care about money because she's got it.* I have to admit, this was so primitive of me because I knew the personal history and struggles of this family through a close relationship with this lady's daughter. Even though I knew some facts, I still wasn't convinced that this woman was telling the truth, but I kept listening. As she continued to talk about her family, she began to speak about her spouse and how he was mean- spirited. Although they made money, it didn't matter because he treated her badly. I listened and tried to understand why she was telling me this.

As she talked I began to realize that she was really sizing me up. She asked about my goals and dreams. She stated that her husband was just like me. And then she said something that I will never forget, something that pierced my heart. She said, "It is not worth it if you don't have someone to share it with." I almost dismissed what she said because, in my mind, she had no point. She had attained financial stability and was already significantly rich. But she continued by emphasizing that she and her husband had everything, but it was never enough for him.

At this point in the conversation, I started catching on to why she was saying this to me. I asked her, "Do you really think I am like your husband?" She pointedly replied, "I know you are and I knew it the first time I met you." "How did you know that?" I asked her. "It was the way you carried yourself, almost like a bully." I was stunned by her answer and told her I thought she was mean, but that did not stop this woman from getting into my mix. She wanted me to know that it is good to have a goal, but her question to me was this, "What will it cost you to achieve it?"

Well, I had to ponder this for a while. I wanted to be rich in terms of millions of dollars, but now I also wanted to define the true meaning of life (being happy, content, and peaceful, no matter what state I am in). As this woman continued to speak about her husband, I cringed with fear thinking that I might eventually become the same way. Although I had never been one to step on people to get what I wanted, I realized I was starting to get there. The other thing she said to me was that I was "insatiable" with my ambitions and feelings. She said her husband was the same way. She said they made the money together. However, she mentioned that making that money wasn't all that enjoyable. She said she had gone through a lot to make that money with her husband and now all she wanted was a job and no big burdens.

This conversation bothered me because I'd always felt that going after money made people have a negative perspective of me. Whenever I would state that I wanted to be rich, most people looked at me like I was crazy. They all acted like they never wanted to be wealthy. Today, I have come to realize that there are people who don't want to be wealthy. I have learned that if you truly want wealth, you don't talk about it, you just go and get it. Talking about money with most people is a sore subject, because most people don't have it and they have a fear of being poor. So often money is associated with greed when it comes to poor people. Money in itself is not evil. In fact, the Good Book says that "the love of money" is the root of all evil.

NUGGET:

People who have problems talking
about money have money problems.

They don't want to speak about their problems because they believe they will go away. I'm here to tell you that your problems will not just go away. To get rid of them requires hard work to make things happen, and faith. I can't speak about other people, but I have to talk about and process my problems in order for them to get better. If you do not talk about your problems, they are not going to magically disappear. In fact, they won't leave at all unless you take a good hard look at them. This woman really had my number because I thought that money would solve a lot of problems. A word to the wise, money can only be used to purchase stuff.

NUGGET:

Money will not fix problems,

it just provides opportunities

for problems to be fixed.

The way problems came into your life is usually the same way to help fix them. For example: You did not become poor because of a lack of money, you became poor because most of your role models were poor. If you had rich parents, you would have practiced the behaviors of the rich. Poor people have characteristics that differ from the other classes of people, such as middle class and rich.

However, the middle class is just what it says – middle class. So, it is "outclassed" by the upper class. This means you're in the middle of the poor and the rich. Have you ever paid attention to the different class levels? In conversations, most of us refer to either the poor or the rich. The middle class has only one distinction: it is in the middle. It is called that because it is average. The thing that's wrong with being average is that people get comfortable there. Please don't get the *other 'aire* confused with the middle class because it is vastly different. Again, the *other 'aire* is a person who has the characteristics of the rich without the money, but the money will come. When that woman the I spoke of was talking with me, I got a little upset because she had bypassed the middle class and I felt she just wanted me to stay there. Later on I realized that she was using our conversation to warn me. I really thanked her that day because she helped make a difference in my life.

Now, I told you that story for a reason, and here's the secret I wanted to give you. I just need you to ask yourself, "Are you ready?" It took me over ten years to learn this, but I finally got it. *Life is not defined in terms of money, but fullness of joy.* One may think that money will do the impossible, but it won't. In fact, it can't. I am totally convinced of that. Having money equals having millions for some people, but not for everyone. Please don't believe the lie that everyone is trying to sell you. *Who Wants to be a Millionaire* is good in theory, but it is only a game show. You need to remember this is real life. Besides, what a million dollars can buy in New York City is substantially less than what it could buy in Kansas City. Living in a major city like New York with its high cost of living will make you lose money, while in Kansas City you may live high on the hog. Simply put, a million dollars in NYC won't buy everything it can buy in KC. Do you have to have a million dollars to be happy and joyful? No! The answer again is definitely no! If you made one hundred thousand dollars a year in the Midwest, you would be just as happy as someone who made a million dollars and lived in New York City, if you managed it well. In most parts of the Midwest, you can buy a house and still have money left over to go shopping and buy furniture, which more than likely you can't do in New York City. Again, the point is to live comfortably, and enjoy your life, not be poor and struggling.

Life is a choice. You have to make a decision to live happily and with joyfulness. No one can make this happen for you. You have to be willing to go to another level in your life. That is what the *other 'aire* is all about. It's not about millionaires or billionaires; it's about all the others. The ones who just want to have more time and freedom to pursue their dreams, and have a desire to make a difference in someone else's life. *Other 'aires* are the richest of all the - aires because they understand the truth of living life. They understand what it truly means to live life to its fullest. So, you won't find these people hanging out in the crack houses or the pawnshops or doing detrimental things to their lives. These are the people who are not afraid to help others. They want to get ahead without stepping on other people. *Other 'aires* are classy individuals. Even millionaires and billionaires can be *other 'aires* if they catch onto the true meaning of life.

Life was meant to be lived to the fullest. We must always strive for enjoyment. No matter what, it will not always be easy being the *other 'aire*. Perhaps after this, you too will become a millionaire or a billionaire. Find your purpose and do what you love if you are to be truly successful in life. Join me and millions of other people in our quest to be greater in our lives. I am an *other 'aire,* what about you? Don't miss out on life by chasing money instead of chasing love, joy, peace, kindness, and the like. These are the things that will truly make a difference at the end of your days. If you're like me, you won't want to look back at your life and have regrets or be tormented because you stepped on people in order to achieve what you thought was "greatness." Instead, you want to have great memories. I encourage you not to wait another minute. If you need help in making a change, don't hesitate to take into account the things I discussed in this book. Be an *other 'aire* in training. Determine to be happy, no matter what life brings.

Make the change today and live the absolutely best life you can. Join me and be an *other 'aire*.

Acknowledge your reality,
but produce great results…

Nuggets of Knowledge

1. Quit beating yourself up because you did not become rich (or whatever else) by a certain age.

2. Life is about exploration and all of us have a purpose; it just takes some of us longer to find ours out.

3. Credit is not a magic pot of gold, but a means to accomplish an end.

4. Sound is to a motion picture what money is to life: it's nice to hear the soundtrack but even better to see the movie!

5. Systems can only take advantage of the ignorance of the ignorant.

6. Learn it, use it, work it, top it.

7. We are all *aires* of something; we just need to figure out what.

8. Most of the time when you hear people speak about something and you respond to it, rarely is it anything new to you. It may be that at this particular moment, you are open to believe it.

9. Don't throw away your old dreams; they are the starting blocks of your greatness.

10. When you find your thing and it feels right, do it!

11. Don't let fear paralyze you; if you do, it will rule you and delay your increase.

12. If you have a belief then stick with it and let it work for you.

13. Fear is like a moat surrounding a castle: once you conquer the moat you will always have access to the castle....

14. The illusion of success may, at times, overshadow the real reality of humble beginnings.

15. Problems seem bigger through the wrong set of lenses.

16. Find partners you can trust who will help you if the going gets tough.

17. Spend most of your time with people who will build you up, not drag you down.

18. Refusing to see the truth now will cost you much more later.

19. Remember, you're poor because of your poor choices.

20. Debt is like a boa constrictor – the more you resist dealing with it, the tighter it squeezes.

21. If you owe it, you don't own it.

22. "Fail" is a verb; therefore you cannot be a failure. Just switch your actions from failure to success.

23. If it is hard to see daylight from inside a tunnel.

24. If Uncle Bubba is a thief, don't take him to your CEO's house party.

25. No press, no success.

26. Never rush progress. Like quicksand, the faster you move the deeper you sink.

27. People who have problems talking about money have money problems.

28. Money will not fix problems; it just provides opportunities for problems to be fixed.

BIBLIOGRAPHY

The Millionaire Real Estate Agent: It's Not About the Money. It's about being the best you can be! By: Gary Keller, Dave Jenks, and Jay Papason.

Rich Dad, Poor Dad: What the Rich Teach Their Kids About Money, That the Poor and Middle Class Don't By: Robert Kiyosaki and Sharon Lechter.

Cashflow Quadrant: Rich Dad's Guide to Financial Freedom By: Robert Kiyosaki and Sharon Lechter.

Dumping Debt: Breaking the Chains of Debt (Financial Peace University) By: Dave Ramsey (Audio CD).

Dr. Farrah Gray: speaking in Buffalo New York (2007).